The Whole School Library
Learning Commons

THE WHOLE SCHOOL LIBRARY LEARNING COMMONS

An Educator's Guide

Judith Anne Sykes

Foreword by David V. Loertscher

LIBRARIES
UNLIMITED™

An Imprint of ABC-CLIO, LLC

Santa Barbara, California • Denver, Colorado

Library of Congress Cataloging-in-Publication Data

Names: Sykes, Judith A., 1957– author.
Title: The whole school library learning commons : an educator's guide /
    Judith Anne Sykes.
Description: Santa Barbara, CA : Libraries Unlimited, [2016] | Includes
    bibliographical references and index.
Identifiers: LCCN 2016013111 (print) | LCCN 2016032581 (ebook) | ISBN
    9781440844201 (paperback) | ISBN 9781440844218 (ebook)
Subjects: LCSH: School libraries—Aims and objectives. | Information commons.
    | Professional learning communities. | School librarian participation in
    curriculum planning. | Teacher-librarians. | Teaching teams. | Mentoring
    in education. | Educational accountability. | Action research in
    education. | School libraries—Canada—Case studies.
Classification: LCC Z675.S3 S957 2016 (print) | LCC Z675.S3 (ebook) | DDC
    025.1/978—dc23
LC record available at https://lccn.loc.gov/2016013111

ISBN: 978-1-4408-4420-1
EISBN: 978-1-4408-4421-8

20 19 18 17 16   1 2 3 4 5

This book is also available as an eBook.

Libraries Unlimited
An Imprint of ABC-CLIO, LLC

ABC-CLIO, LLC
130 Cremona Drive, P.O. Box 1911
Santa Barbara, California 93116-1911
www.abc-clio.com

This book is printed on acid-free paper ∞

Manufactured in the United States of America

To Whole School Library Learning Commons Teams everywhere.
And to Bob, Michelle, Billy, Joey, and Oscar.

CONTENTS

Foreword   *ix*
  David V. Loertscher

Preface   *xi*

Acknowledgments   *xv*

Introduction   *xvii*

Part I: Mentoring the WSLLC

Chapter 1: Mentoring for Implementation and Sustainability   3

Chapter 2: Selected Mentoring Resources with Strategies   15

Chapter 3: Mentoring Case Studies   31

Part II: Accountability for Learning and WSLLC

Chapter 4: Authentic Accountability, Standards, and Policies   45

Chapter 5: Selected Accountability Resources with Strategies   59

Part III: Reading and Research on WSLLC

Chapter 6: School Library to Learning Commons Literature
                and Research   77

Chapter 7: Selected Learning Commons Literature and Research
                with Strategies   89

Part IV: Community and WSLLC

Chapter 8:   Engaging Community   109

Chapter 9:   Selected Resources with Strategies for Community
                   Engagement   121

                   Bibliography   *135*

                   Index   *145*

FOREWORD

The idea of the learning commons, not yet quite a decade old, was to transform the idea of a school library stocked with resources repository into a vibrant and central component of teaching and learning in the school community. Thus, the name change to focus on "learning" and its participatory community idea centered in "commons." For most schools, the stereotypical notion of a circulating book collection has been difficult to transform and continues to resist any other function even in the drastic change in the world of information and technology. Some have interpreted the idea of the learning commons as a simple rearrangement of furniture in an existing physical facility or just adding a few computers to the mix.

In her current book, Judith Sykes, who has worked a great deal on the concept and contributed much to its success, advocates not just a single room or space in the school but a transformation of the entire school both in the physical and the virtual sense. She recognizes the power of a vibrant learning community that takes advantage of information and technology in all its forms and recognizes that children and teens now live in a very different world than the previous generation and must be prepared to compete globally in what they know and are able to do.

This book is not for the beginner. Rather, it is for administrators, department heads, teachers, librarians, and parents who may have been introduced to the idea but may be struggling to expand the concept and its impact throughout the school. Readers of this work will be introduced to the idea of the learning commons as the extension of each classroom, the cross-classroom connection, and the center of active learning that extends beyond the school.

Before reading this work, readers should digest the recent Canadian standards, *Leading Learning: Standards of Practice for School Library Learning Commons in Canada* (Canadian Library Association [CLA], 2014b), development coordinated by Judith Sykes and Carol Koechlin for CLA. Then as a group of leaders in the school, use this book with its very practical planning guides and recommendations to develop a vision for a whole school learning commons and carry it out. Such an effort transforms a static entity into an incredible active learning opportunity for everyone.

Teachers begin to feel that they are not alone in the isolated classroom pushing mastery enough to pass tests. Parents begin to realize that their children are not just filling assignments but are involved in real and challenging experiences that give them a much clearer vision of their potential in a changed world. Gradually, administrators are able to articulate and demonstrate what a whole school learning community looks like, feels like, and a whole that is much greater than the sum of a bunch of parts pieced together.

Judith has crossed international borders in her writing in a good way that suggests to the reader how differing systems and cultures can embrace the distinctive environment of a learning commons. We can explore differing perspectives as we create our own vision of a learning commons environment for a particular school. The best perspective here is that it takes many heads in the school, not just a single person, to think, experiment, and create an entirely different learning environment. This book sends the reader to a host of resources to use and strategies to build and create a fascinating and exemplary learning community. Congratulations, Judith!

David V. Loertscher

PREFACE

Dear Educator,

Do you like to collaborate on an innovative learning approach that involves you and your students in deep thinking and learning of curriculum, knowledge building, collaboration, success, and enjoyment? Have you heard about achieving this through expanding the pedagogical practices of your school library program into a whole school learning commons? This book is a guide, informing you about the pedagogical shift occurring as school libraries move towards a learning commons approach, and how to implement and sustain the approach to impact student learning success.

After completing a book focused on site-based action research to examine school library programs (Sykes, 2013), I served as project coordinator and contributing writer for new school library standards for the Canadian Library Association (CLA). This involved engaging committees across the country whose members represented an ideal school library learning commons steering team. The result, *Leading Learning: Standards of Practice for School Library Learning Commons in Canada* (Canadian Library Association, 2014b), was launched at Treasure Mountain Canada 3 (Treasure Mountain Canada, 2016), an extension of United States Treasure Mountain Research Retreats developed by David Loertscher and colleagues in 1989 to focus on school library research as a valuable catalyst for school improvement, based on contributions and analysis of research in the field (Loertscher, 2015c).

These new Canadian standards are not a revision of former standards, *Achieving Information Literacy, Standards for School Library Programs in Canada* (Asselin et al., 2003), supported and published by CLA and a seminal reference on its own, but provide a new digital format focused on changing landscapes in education and the entire library community, centered on the school library learning commons philosophy as a whole school pedagogical culture. Thinking about how such standards are implemented and sustained throughout schools, I contributed an article to TMC3, where I consider implementing and sustaining a whole school library learning commons through the developmental concepts of mentoring, accountability, research, and community (Sykes, 2014).

In related events on school library learning commons development, such as workshops and webinars that I conduct, I am often asked about why and how schools move from a school library to a school library learning commons. What is the difference? What does it mean for a school? What is a learning commons? I begin exploring these types of questions with the following learning commons definitions:

> A learning commons is a whole school approach to building a participatory learning community. The library learning commons is the physical and virtual collaborative learning hub of the school. It is designed to engineer and drive future-oriented learning and teaching throughout the entire school. Inquiry, project/problem-based learning experiences are designed as catalysts for intellectual engagement with information, ideas, thinking, and dialogue. Reading thrives, learning literacies and technology competencies evolve, and critical thinking, creativity, innovation and playing to learn are nourished. Everyone is a learner; everyone is a teacher working collaboratively toward excellence. (Canadian Library Association, 2014b, p. 5)

> A Learning Commons is a common or shared space that is both physical and virtual. It is designed to move students beyond mere research, practice and group work to a greater level of engagement through exploration, experimentation, and collaboration. A Learning Commons is more than a room or a website. A Learning Commons allows users to create their own environments to improve learning. A Learning Commons is about changing school culture, and transforming the way teaching and learning occur. (Loertscher, Koechlin, and Rosenfeld, 2012, p. 1)

The move from school library to learning commons often begins with schools modernizing their physical school library space and web page, thinking that this modernization is now somehow not a school library (what was wrong with that?) but a "learning commons," with new paint, signs, flexible furnishings, shelves, and an increase in digital resources. This is a good start, but students, staff members, and parents find this confusing, unaware that the change occurring is to enable the pedagogy of the learning commons approach to make an impact on learning and teaching. Environment is important, as brain research (Sykes, 2006) informs us; basic physical needs must be met for optimal learning—nutrition, hydration, exercise—along with how learning spaces work better. Many high schools are starting to incorporate "coffee houses" within newly renovated school library learning commons, or "allow" students to bring in water bottles or healthy snacks. Great ideas, but do experiential, relevant, and intellectual learning needs thrive? Learning commons pedagogy incorporates both physical and virtual realms where students and teachers are welcomed, focused on learning, and able to connect and communicate locally and globally. Chris Kennedy, Superintendent of Schools, West Vancouver School District, British Columbia, writes: "While the physical spaces are exciting, the changes to our mindsets are far more powerful" (Kennedy, 2015).

The focus of a learning commons approach is learning. Best practice necessitates a whole school approach, to ascertain a cultural shift in thinking, learning, and teaching, and it is challenging to implement this learning and teaching "revolution" (Loertscher, 2008). The principal, teacher-librarians, other administrators, and teachers need to understand the whys and how of implementing the school-wide approach together to make the shift. Meeting student learning needs, along with mandated curriculum, informs and moves the "whole school library learning commons" forward. Educators comment that when they understand the key background information and can access available implementation tools regarding the learning commons approach, they are invigorated and excited, and see how it reflects practice they currently try to lead, change, or implement.

Student learning needs vary from school to school and over time, and require ongoing collective analysis at each school, which involves examining data from broad-based assessment—test results, report cards, projects, and daily work—to look for patterns and themes. These patterns and themes provide a picture as to what instructional and resource-based designs can best support students through the learning commons approach. The pedagogical shift is succinctly summarized in figure P.1, "Pedagogical Shifts Inherent in the Learning Commons."

Many educators are unaware of school library best practice, never mind learning commons development and best practice, as neither is often mentioned in graduate or post-graduate education degrees or in district activities or priorities. This is due to factors such as perception and finances—the school library is viewed as a traditional, rather costly resource center—or memories of the school library as a quiet place full of books rather than an active environment integral to learning throughout the school. Many educators are unaware of the learning commons potential as change agent and driver of transforming learning and teaching, in

Information Seeking and Reporting		Individual and Collective Knowledge Creation
Teacher-directed learning	➥	Self and participatory learning
Classroom learning	➥	Networked and global learning
Standards-driven	➥	Exploring big ideas and concepts
Teaching	➥	Process and active learning
Individual teacher expertise	➥	Collaborative learning partnerships

Figure P.1 Pedagogical Shifts Inherent in the Learning Commons (Ontario School Library Association, 2010, p. 35)

addition to its ability to inspire lifelong learning and literacy. As a former principal, assistant principal, teacher-librarian, and teacher, I wrote this book as a guide for educators for leading, understanding, and implementing the whole school library learning commons approach, encouraging a cultural shift in learning and teaching by exploring its implementation through synergistic planning, goal-setting, and actions involving the principal, teacher-librarian, other administrators, specialists, and teachers, engaging the learning community in an exciting, empowering approach to impact student learning.

Sincerely,
Judith Sykes

ACKNOWLEDGMENTS

When writing a book about the whole school library learning commons, acknowledgement must be given to the pioneers, experts, and educational leaders who created the evolution, Dr. David V. Loertscher and Carol Koechlin, who have and continue to publish and speak extensively and tirelessly as "global mentors," inspiring educators around the world in adapting or adopting the school library to learning commons approach. In turn, their impact on student learning is phenomenal.

INTRODUCTION

The village green, or "common," was traditionally a place to graze livestock, stage a festival, or meet neighbors. This concept of social utility underlies the philosophy of the modern learning commons, which is a flexible environment built to accommodate multiple learning activities. Designing—or redesigning—a commons starts with an analysis of student needs and the kind of work they will be doing. (Lippincott and Greenwall, 2011)

Prior to leading, championing, implementing, supporting, and sustaining a learning community in adopting a whole school library learning commons (WSLLC) pedagogy, educators pose and answer questions such as the following:

- What is different about a school library and the WSLLC approach?
- Why do we all need to be involved in this?
- Is this another "buzzword" or passing trend?
  And, most importantly
- How does this help meet the complex learning needs of students?

To help address and explore these questions, this book is written as a guide for educators in leading, implementing, and sustaining the approach, by framing it around four developmental concepts—mentoring, accountability, research, and community—that each educator takes a part in. Although each developmental concept is presented in four distinct parts in this book, they function and interact with each other on a continual basis and within the actions of the principal, other administrators or specialists in the school, teacher-librarian, and all of the teachers. (The term "teacher-librarian" is used throughout this book synonymous with "school librarian" or "media specialist," and denotes having certification as a teacher as well as education in school librarianship—e.g., specialist diploma, Master of Education, Master of Library and Information Science.)

The first letters of the developmental concepts form the acronym MARC, which to librarians means "machine-readable cataloging." MARC is also an acronym to assist in remembering and using the developmental concepts and strategies of Mentoring, Accountability, Research, and Community, when immersed in conducting the busy daily work of schools, school libraries, and transformation to the learning commons approach.

Prior to introducing each developmental concept of MARC for the approach in this book, I ask readers to keep the following understandings in mind:

- Best practice in school library programs led to the emergence of the whole school library learning commons pedagogy. Although this book will include some school library background and information, as pertinent to the learning commons approach, we will focus primarily on learning commons.
- School library programs in some districts meet with budget reductions. Some schools have teacher-librarians who lead or champion the learning commons approach; some don't have them or are at risk of losing them. This book includes strategies, ideas, and scenarios for overcoming reductions by moving educators forward collectively with the WSLLC and the concept of steering teams.
- What if a school is already implementing the approach? Great! This book contains tools and strategies to assess and reflect on the journey, so that schools can keep growing, adapt to new students and faculty, meet other challenges, and keep getting better. The WSLLC is a pedagogy of continual learning and growth.

Each part of the book discusses one particular developmental concept in context of the approach and how the concept is important to developing the approach. This is followed by highlighting key resources with strategies relevant to that concept, which educators can share and use in supporting the change. Many of the suggested strategies and actions pertain to each educator's role in the process—for example, what strategies or actions does the principal engage in to mentor teachers in the approach? How does the principal lead the staff in demonstrating accountability in learning, to ensure that their efforts continually impact and enhance student learning? What key references or resources does the principal know about to prepare self and faculty for the innovation? How does the principal support or conduct action research at the school relating to the transformation? How does the principal engage the community in the cultural shift? What about the teacher-librarian and the other school administrators, such as the vice principal or department heads and all of the teachers?

For the WSLLC approach to propel and support a dynamic culture of learning and teaching, the entire learning community must be part of the discussion, actions, and processes. All school staff members, especially school library staff such as library technicians or library clerical staff, are part of the development and members of steering teams. Student and parent representation on steering teams or involvement in other ways is critical to development. Involving librarians from the community, district specialists, and other partners or organizations involved with the school is vital. Community is the focus of the fourth part of the book, highlighting ways and means for educators to engage the learning community.

DEVELOPMENTAL CONCEPTS

The first developmental concept presented in this book, *mentoring*, is an art that takes patience and skill. Its objective is to guide others in thinking and to facilitate shared understandings or approaches. Without mentoring and its various approaches (coaching, informing, consulting, collaborating, reflecting), what often occurs is that when key leaders leave—such as the principal or teacher-librarian, who guide and steer the innovation—developments cease. However, if mentoring—or, at the least, quality transition preparation—occurs to prepare new leaders, and shared ownership is built with the learning community, this facilitates continuity of growth, along with the incorporation of fresh ideas and talent. Co-teaching and collaboration are key components of mentoring the learning commons approach. Five cases studies relating to learning commons mentoring are included for study and discussion.

The second developmental concept, *accountability*, encompasses the documentation of evidence relating to the effectiveness of the WSLLC pedagogical approach upon student learning over time—accountability for learning. Ultimately, the purpose of an effective WSLLC is to inclusively support all students in the school through the learning goals and outcomes of the ministries of education. For this to occur, the learning commons plans, goals, strategies, and actions form part of the overall school plan, based on the needs of each student as identified through ongoing, varied student data collection and analysis. This means negotiating each student's learning profile with mandated curriculum, and involving educators working together to co-plan, design, teach, and assess learning experiences. It is not about trying to fit students and curriculum into artificially created environments or collections; it is about ensuring that collections and resources throughout the school are developed to support co-determined student needs. This part of the book presents strategies for schools to collectively focus on the significant questions in moving forward:

- How does the approach support each student's learning?
- How do we know it does?

Once most practitioners work in schools, *research* often becomes a distant memory from university study. The third developmental concept, research, presents key literature and research informing the emergence of the learning commons approach. School-based, on-site research, or action research, is discussed, which is now accepted as being at the center of school improvement and a peak professional development activity for teachers. School-based action research does not need to be time consuming or "yet another thing to do"; it is a way of thinking about teaching and learning that is reflective, data-based, and cyclical, supporting continual pedagogical growth and development. When implementing the learning commons approach, action research in accountability for learning allows schools to examine the following issues:

- What is working?
- What isn't?
- What do we do next?
- What do we stop doing? Start doing? Do differently?
- What insights do others offer us?

The fourth developmental concept presented in this book, *community*, is the most vital; without it, implementing—and especially sustaining—the WSLLC approach is virtually impossible. In the spirit of professional learning communities, collaborative teams steering the WSLLC approach facilitate responsibility and ownership of it as a cultural shift throughout a learning community. Everyone is welcomed to the process, contributes, and learns.

Figure I.1 illustrates the concepts, how they interact, and how they benefit WSLLC development.

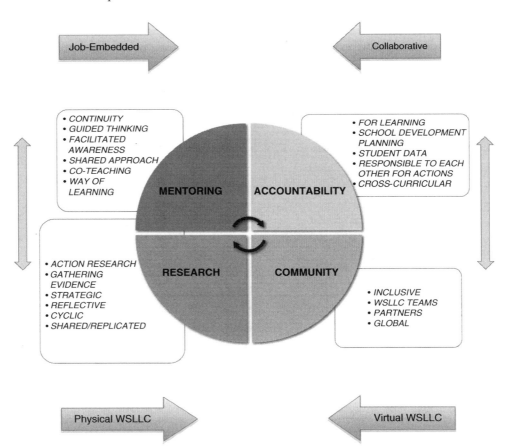

Figure I.1 Whole School Library Learning Commons Development Concepts: Key Understandings

Ultimately, through mentoring, accountability, research, and community, implementing and sustaining the WSLLC approach involves educators creating rich, active learning experiences and environments to benefit student learning. When describing an effective learning commons, which encompasses both physical and virtual spaces, most experts in the field and educational leaders agree that they envision lively, busy spaces inhabited by students engaged in a variety of learning experiences. They describe comfortable, welcoming spaces filled with dialogue, collaborative knowledge-building, and activity, which also have areas for reading, reflection, and study. Most important of all is seeing the spaces constantly inhabited by students learning and doing, with educators guiding, facilitating, and coaching. This book will focus on resources and strategies that lead to developing environments such as these, through educators collectively engaging in:

- Developing and reviewing the WSLLC plan;
- Forming a steering team;
- Basing planning on the collective analysis of student learning data;
- Sharing the plan with the learning community;
- Setting pedagogical and budget goals in stages;
- Knowing and keeping current on the literature, research, policies, and standards;
- Demonstrating accountability through site-based action research;
- Celebrating successes and continuing to grow;
- Connecting with others who are on the journey.

Three Keys to Unlock the WSLLC

- Active leadership of the principal
- Co-teaching and collaboration
- Base on student need, from student data

Part I

MENTORING THE WSLLC

Chapter 1

MENTORING FOR IMPLEMENTATION AND SUSTAINABILITY

Collaborative learning cultures in schools and boards are characterized by educators' learning from each other as they work together with a common focus on improved student achievement and well-being. Mentoring can foster a collaborative learning culture within schools and school boards by building capacity for the skills and approaches that contribute to shared learning and professional dialogue. (Ontario Leadership Strategy, 2011, p. 9)

The whole school library learning commons (WSLLC) depends upon a collaborative learning culture to thrive and impact student learning, and mentoring is an important part of fostering this culture. Mentoring is an art in itself that takes patience, aptitude, and proficiency, and is used and learned in a variety of formal and informal ways as educators collaborate to develop the WSLLC. The objective of mentoring is to guide others in thinking and facilitate shared understandings or approaches. For many educators, this is a new approach to a way of designing instruction and thinking about the school library as a whole school learning commons. "Mentoring usually refers to non-evaluative relationships maintained over time between a newer and a more experienced professional, and is often offered to an individual who is new to a position. The focus is the professional learning needs of the mentee" (Ontario Leadership Strategy, 2011, p. 10). Discovering what professional learning an individual needs and how to select mentoring strategies suited to what is required for the approach to be successful is critical to the approach having an impact on student learning.

The learning commons pedagogy focuses on student achievement of curricular learning goals and outcomes successfully and equitably from the collective efforts of the professional learning community, who analyze and interpret student learning data through broad-based assessment. Mentoring becomes an effective developmental concept for creating shared understanding about approaching instructional design in the learning commons, through the focus on student context. Even in schools well on the way to effectively implementing the approach, without mentoring both current and new educators on-site, the growth of the approach is set back or even abandoned as the educators who led the development—such as the principal and/or teacher-librarian—move on to other schools or positions. This is particularly true if the concept is viewed by other educators in the school or incoming leaders appointed to the school as yet another "new thing" that did not "catch on" and is not embedded in a collaborative culture of learning and teaching throughout the school. Facilitating a collaborative culture of learning and teaching, through formal and informal mentoring approaches and strategies, works toward ensuring that the implementation and sustainability of the approach is a continual process of growing educational practice and improving student learning success. Without ongoing mentoring, many of the superb resources, articles, research findings, models, and strategies foundational to and supporting the approach don't get read or used or provide sustainability ideas for growth; ownership of the approach is viewed as an interest of a few individuals. Some students gain greatly in thriving collaborative learning cultures, and others without such learning cultures do not gain to the same extent.

Many successful organizations and corporations provide mentoring programs when transitioning new leaders or bringing new employees into the organization. In educational practice, several programs and organizations support student mentoring, mentoring for new principals, new teachers, and, while not as many, mentoring programs for new teacher-librarians noted further in this chapter. Educators new to a learning community bring fresh talents and ideas to the community; mentorship eases the transition for them as they join the new school community. Through mentoring, continuing members of the learning community, beyond welcoming new members and their contributions into the established community, support continuity into the efforts that the community built, measured, and wishes to further, especially if they themselves were mentored by departing members and if they share ownership of the approach.

Important elements for mentorship honor the principles of effective professional development, which include interacting with colleagues in a "nurturing environment … job embedded and relevant" (Brown, Dotson, and Yontz, 2011, p. 57). In the development of the learning commons approach, these elements begin with the principal, who knows and understands how this pedagogy impacts student learning and teaching practices, and then facilitates multiple approaches of mentoring tailored to the strengths and needs of the faculty. As the initiative progresses, the principal ensures that educators learn from each other using a variety of mentorship approaches. The importance of the principal's role in implementing and sustaining best practice has its roots in extensive global research and studied practice demonstrating the principal's role in the active support of effective school library programs over time (Henri, Hay, and Oberg, 2002). As school libraries transform, the principal continues to make the significant difference to success and cannot be emphasized enough as the learning commons approach evolves to present a dynamic method for school reform with the promise it delivers to impact student success.

Principals exploring or beginning to implement the approach seek out mentoring from other principals or teacher-librarian colleagues who forge ahead with implementation, or, if forging forward, become mentors themselves to other principals or to a new principal replacing them if they move from the school. The mentoring happens in a variety of formal or informal ways, from a timely phone call or conversation after a district meeting, to the more formal formation of district discussion groups at principal meetings or among feeder schools within a community. Feeder schools within a community consider exploring the learning commons approach together to develop continuity as students move from elementary school through to senior high school. Principals also mentor the other administrators and specialists on-site at the school, and take an active role in forming and mentoring the WSLLC steering teams.

In working to create this type of a participatory learning culture through the learning commons approach, principals and other educators may find mentorship challenging. One reason for this is unfamiliarity with the background, literature, and student impact studies regarding effective school library programs now developing into the learning commons pedagogy. This information is scarce in educational degree work or district work. It appears that school library impact study evidence is "ignored" as a number of schools or districts cut back on school libraries and the leadership of teacher-librarians (Oberg, 2014a). Another reason is that school library student impact studies or information do not surface in the complex work of educators, who must balance many agendas, policies, and roles in striving to meet the diverse learning needs of all of the students and the expectations of the district and the community. Educators lead and advocate for students on many levels with available and often scarce resources. Instructional leaders such as principals, other school administrators, and teacher-librarians teach assigned core subjects, cover planning time, act as resource teachers, coach teams, and involve themselves in many other activities depending on the nature of the school. This is dichotomous, as the ultimate goal of schools is that all students succeed with focus on learning and teaching best practice, yet the school library and learning commons impact seems new and unheard of. Yet another reason is that transforming a school library to a learning commons is considered a superfluous expense when the budget is tight. Educators need to view this transformative approach as a sound investment first and foremost, founded on collaborative instructional design based on identified student need, rather than focusing on funding or modernizing a facility or purchasing additional resources. These things come in time once the learning approach is in motion. The essence of success is to keep the focus on learning and collaborative instructional design, followed by planning for outcome-based resources and spaces determined by student need. Through mentoring, principals and other educators grow to understand why processes of collaborative planning, teaching, and assessing based on collective analysis of student need are highly effective, and how they support and enhance teaching practice and ultimately impact student success.

Mentoring has always been and continues to be an essential component of the role of an effective teacher-librarian. Teacher-librarians expand and "explode" the school library program beyond its confines when using a learning commons approach: taking it from a place full of things to an active, vibrant learning approach. Teacher-librarian certification, and an educator's suitability for the teacher-librarian specialty, incorporates developing and employing mentoring techniques on a variety of continuous levels. A teacher-librarian collaborates with and often mentors the principal, other administrators, and teachers, in the introduction and demonstration of collaborative instructional design and co-teaching based on co-analysis of student learning profiles central to the purpose of moving forward and engaging with the learning commons approach. In many schools a teacher-librarian will initiate the transformation, and if that teacher-librarian moves on without having mentored other educators for continuity and sustainability of the evolving approach, the development of the approach is jeopardized. Sometimes, due to budget reasons in the case of an effective teacher-librarian, the teacher-librarian is not even to be replaced. It is important for teacher-librarians, leading and mentoring a thriving learning commons approach, to mentor like-minded teachers who share interest in leadership in the event that the teacher-librarian leaves the school, potentially creating a desire for such interested teachers to certify as teacher-librarians in the future. If the teacher-librarian is being replaced by another teacher-librarian, the former mentor at minimum spends quality transition time with the latter as they move into the position from the individual who is leaving. Teacher-librarians mentor the library support staff members, such as library technicians, assistants, or clerks, assuring them of their vital role in supporting learning commons implementation and what changes mean for them, including their importance in serving on the WSLLC steering team. Teacher-librarians also mentor the steering team and other teacher-librarians in the district.

Whether new to the teacher-librarian role or to the learning commons approach, teacher-librarians themselves seek mentorship. The American Association of School Librarians (AASL) recognizes several resources for mentoring programs focused on the teacher-librarian (American Association of School Librarians, 2016b). AASL recommends that new teacher-librarians, or teachers interested in the role, contact a school with an experienced teacher-librarian or the state or provincial school library professional organization (or other professional organizations, like technology organizations), to arrange a preliminary visit to a potential mentee's site. An example of a formal teacher-librarian mentorship program was an arrangement supported by the New Jersey Association of School Librarians (NJASL), to "assign an established Mentor for one year to work with a new School Library Media Specialist to help acclimate them on how to effectively operate and support a school library media program ... based on the three central ideas from *Information Power*: collaboration, leadership, and technology" (NJASL, 2013).

The Maine State Library provides online lists with contact information from experienced teacher-librarians who volunteer as school library mentors, including mentors willing to provide guidance in collaborating with teachers, which is challenging to both new and experienced teacher-librarians; however, it is fundamental to effective teacher-librarianship (Maine State Library, 2015). Formal teacher-librarian mentorship programs created in Maryland, Iowa, Georgia, and Virginia had "specific criteria for defining and selecting mentors for teacher-librarians," including experience, personality, communication skills, interest, and commitment to the process and relationship. They "referenced their data to remark on the success of these mentoring programs and to highlight the benefits that came to mentors, mentees, and school districts involved" (Maliszewski, 2016, p. 9). The Toronto, Ontario, District School Board (TDSB) offers a variety of professional learning methods and tools as mentoring supports for new and practicing teacher-librarians, such as "group mentoring, informal mentoring, and online mentoring" (Maliszewski, 2016, p. 6). York University in Toronto aimed a Mentorship Additional Qualification course at TDSB teachers. This course was experienced by teacher-librarian Maliszewski when mentoring a new teacher-librarian, where she discovered the benefits firsthand of both mentor and mentee becoming better teachers (Maliszewski, 2016).

The variety of formal or informal mentoring approaches benefitting the learning commons concept development is ongoing and eventually embeds within school culture, to move toward developing the concept beyond perceptions of championing or advocacy of the school library, into an inclusive, innovative, and energizing whole-school approach to learning and teaching. Mentoring approaches ideally suited to schools and applicable to implementation and sustainability of the learning commons approach involve the following components:

Coaching generally refers to a short-term relationship involving conversations that support job-embedded learning. The goal is set largely by the person being coached and typically has specific outcomes, such as enhancing performance, reflecting on practice, or examining and solving a problem.

Consulting involves one or more individuals who provide expert information, resources, and guidance to others based on the specific knowledge or skills of the consultant(s).

Collaborating is the equitable and collegial process of working together to identify and achieve goals.

Facilitation processes strategically support groups to achieve their goals.
(Ontario Leadership Strategy, 2011, p. 10)

Collaboration is the mentoring cornerstone of the learning commons approach, especially collaborative planning, teaching, and assessment of learning projects and experiences. It is important to have a great facility and superb print and digital collections to support learning and teaching, but co-teaching, ideally with a teacher-librarian, has been proven to have the greatest effect on student learning in the school library research impact studies: "More than 20 studies in the United States and Canada … examined the role and presence of the teacher-librarian in high-performing schools, concluding that teacher-librarian time, schedules and collaboration with teaching colleagues were associated with higher test score outcomes" (Haycock, 2011, p. 38). Collaboration for designing, teaching, and assessing instruction is key to impacting student success yet, as noted, is one of the most challenging activities for many teacher-librarians, new or experienced, as well as for many teachers. Co-teaching is a key area for mentoring and coaching teachers.

A recent definition of collaborative teaching states, "One or more classroom teachers and/or one or more learning specialists (e.g., teacher-librarian, learning commons teacher) plan, teach, coach and assess a learning event together. Library technicians and/or assistants or support staff work with teachers to support a learning event as directed by the teachers" (Canadian Library Association, 2014b, p. 2). As the implementation of the approach progresses, other administrators and specialists in schools—such as vice principals, technology teachers, reading teachers, guidance counselors, art teachers, and others depending on the context of the school—involve themselves in collaborative teaching experiences. Some "house" their offices in the learning commons physical space, readably fostering and participating in collaborative practice with the other teachers and the teacher-librarian: "In the learning commons, the library functions as a dynamic arena where librarians, reading specialists, and classroom teachers bring individual talents to the instructional process in a co-teaching team" (Parrott and Keith, 2015, p. 12). Co-teaching strives to take the isolation out of teaching and facilitates cooperative, collaborative culture: "The librarian, who co-teaches with the reading specialist and classroom teacher in the learning commons, is taking collaboration to a new and progressive level. In the co-teaching model, each educator offers specialized expertise to augment instruction that distinguishes students' learning styles, thereby maximizing reading and literacy achievement. Differentiating instruction in the learning commons need not entail major renovations or monumental changes" (Parrott and Keith, 2015, p. 17).

Principals provide mentorship and expectations to the teacher-librarian and teachers as they move into co-teaching, to facilitate moving teaching away from deeply rooted isolated practice. Many teachers have not experienced co-teaching, especially with a teacher-librarian. Principals support collaborative practice through flexibly scheduled timetables and common planning time for teachers with teacher-librarians. The principal is responsible for ensuring that co-teaching occurs as the approach moves forward, that teachers, teacher-librarians, and library support staff understand the impact co-teaching has on student success and professional practice development. Principals consult with resident expertise, such as a teacher-librarian if the school employs one on faculty, or accesses consultation from district specialists or experts in the field:

> Evaluating collaborative planning, teaching and assessment, the principal must ensure that the teacher-librarian or learning commons lead teacher models an understanding of the various ways collaborative planning, teaching and assessment can be applied throughout the school and assess if the faculty generally accepts co-teaching, noting the number of collaboratively planned and taught experiences that occur each semester, and providing or seeking methods of professional development

to support its acceptance and growth. This could involve inviting teams co-teaching effectively to do professional development sessions with their departments, other teachers, or other schools and encouraging the presentation of co-taught projects at staff meetings, parent meetings, in school newsletters, and on the school web site linking to the virtual learning commons. (Brown and Sykes, 2016)

During the teacher supervision process, principals dialogue with educators about co-teaching and provide positive feedback of the use of collaborative planning, teaching, and assessing in teacher evaluations.

Teacher-librarians often begin collaborative practice in their school with a handful of like-minded teachers, or even just one other teacher, to set the process in motion. They share and celebrate collaborative practice results within the school at staff meetings, at professional events, and in the physical and virtual commons spaces. This results in the demand for co-teaching learning experiences to grow and involve most or all the faculty over time, as not only do student impact outcomes occur but the professional growth and enjoyment of co-teaching prospers. Co-teaching partners or teams share joint experiences and labor, tend to be more creative, and provide honest, constructive feedback to each other as relationships and trust grow in the process—and students benefit by having access to two or more teachers to know, guide, and support their learning needs.

Educators practice co-taught learning experiences throughout the school, as teachers, teacher-librarians, specialists, and administrators work together with students in the physical school library learning commons, in knowledge-building spaces in the virtual commons, in classrooms, and extending to off-campus field trips. The school library or classroom no longer has "four walls." As part of a district- and university-supported collaborative inquiry project, a teacher-librarian who is also the vice-principal, together with classroom teachers in a K–8 public school, "examined the impact of various ways of eliciting collaboration between the teacher-librarian and classroom teacher and how that impacts the attitudes and willingness of classroom teachers to collaborate with the teacher librarian" (Greater Essex County District School Board and University of Windsor, 2014–2015, p. 34). With principal support, including common planning time for teachers to plan with the teacher-librarian, and district and university study support, a research project was created to determine how "an inviting, accessible learning commons space" and "opportunities provided for collaboration" impact student information literacy skills. The research theory of action assumed the following propositions:

- If the Teacher-Librarian creates an inviting, accessible school library learning commons, then teachers and students will access the space, the resources and the Teacher-Librarian more often.
- If the Teacher-Librarian creates opportunities, then the classroom teachers will collaborate with the Teacher-Librarian.
- If the Teacher-Librarian collaborates with the classroom teacher, then student achievement of information literacy skills will improve.

(Greater Essex County District School Board and
University of Windsor, 2014–2015, p. 34)

These assumptions were not without challenges, for previously at the school "only three out of 12 surveyed teachers worked with a Teacher-Librarian prior to 2014/15" (Greater Essex County District School Board and University of Windsor, 2014–2015, p. 37). Yet the project proved successful on many counts: once teachers "became familiar with the Teacher-Librarian and the Teacher-Librarian became familiar with teachers' methods of instruction, partnership becomes easier" (Greater Essex County District School Board and University of Windsor, 2014–2015, p. 39). Teachers who planned with the teacher-librarian expressed interest to continue the following year and felt that both they and their students had benefitted from the experience.

General steps to successful mentoring through collaborative planning, teaching, and assessing are summarized below:

1. Establish rapport
2. Identify your teaching styles and use them to create a cohesive classroom
3. Discuss strengths and weaknesses
4. Discuss individualized education plans and regular education goals
5. Formulate a plan of action and act as a unified team
6. Take risks and grow ... enjoy

(Marston, 2002)

Although implementation and sustainability of the learning commons approach significantly depend on the principal, school district mentorship is an important and increasing factor. School districts and state, provincial, or territorial departments or organizations often feature mentoring possibilities for educators, but few offer mentoring in leading the learning commons approach, especially for principals. Principals require time to talk to other principals about many aspects of leading schools, including why this approach is significant to school improvement. Districts unfamiliar with the learning commons pedagogical approach invite consultants or teacher-librarians with the expertise to speak to district leaders and principal groups. They discuss the possibilities and challenges of using the approach to impact or reform learning and teaching in their schools. In Fairfield County, Connecticut, Cooperative Educational Services launched a two-year school library to learning commons project, titled "Re-Imagining the School Library," which brought together district teams from 14 school districts representing 133 schools, "to engage in a series of professional learning workshops, planning, guidance, and sharing their successes around the same mission: to transform their school library into a learning commons.... By the end of year one, teams will have developed a shared vision, a district action plan including scope of work, time line and accountability, a collection of data, resources, and strategies to inform the school-based teamwork in the second year" (Kompar, 2015, pp. 20, 22). When former Alberta principal Greg Miller became assistant superintendent of his school division, he set a goal to bring "principals, librarians and teachers on board in such a way that they see the shift to a Learning Commons not as an add on, but rather as a way to support the initiatives that are already underway in our district," and organized a school library learning commons specialist to speak to principals. He invited interested principals to pilot effective implementation, arranged webinars for the pilot schools to participate in, and visited each school to engage in conversation about moving forward (Miller, 2013). Northern Gateway Public Schools (NGPS), Alberta, superintendent Kevin Andrea emphasizes school library learning commons as a model for all NGPS district schools in his opening message to the district: "As learning environments change, so too are the traditional models for school libraries. A learning commons is an inclusive, flexible, learner-centered, physical and/or virtual space for collaboration, inquiry, imagination and play to expand and deepen learning. It is more a perspective than a 'place.' A learning commons perspective supports a student-centered approach that emphasizes active and collaborative engagement, and is a model all NGPS schools are working toward" (Andrea, 2015).

School area or district networks also provide mentorship, and many school districts support "networks of practice" to meet regularly in a variety of ways. Districts with established school library networks bring the learning commons approach to their study or mentorship groups, as networks often provide mentorship in current literature and practices. Schools without school library networks of practice formulate proposals to the area or district to form one. Although networks today have a virtual extension through a website with blogs for discussion, meeting in person, particularly with many educators new to learning commons roles and concept, enables them to build mentoring relationships and feel more comfortable as they get to know each other and engage in open dialogue, posing questions and sharing challenges and successes that carry over to virtual activities such as blogging. Having a mentoring network nearby allows participants to discuss timely topics or issues pertinent to their district or school context as well as broader topics in the field. Network meetings provide opportunity to share current projects and learning events happening in schools, which inspire cross-school projects or mentoring. Network meetings include mentoring activities such as simulated coaching sessions around collaborative planning and teaching, contributing knowledge about new professional resources, standards or policies, and sharing key learning from conferences or workshops that others did not attend.

Networks of practice strive to meet every six to eight weeks so that between meetings members can try out advice, ideas, new information, and resources from meetings. Participants who have connected as mentors/mentees meet or contact each other between sessions if working on a particular strategy, issue, or project together. It seems that in-person network meetings invariably occur after school, difficult for some members to attend. Those in current networks, or when proposing a new district network, ideally benefit from some release of duty time at the start or end of the school day. In some districts this is possible, perhaps offering a half-day release of duty to meet a few times during the school year. In another scenario members meet on the way to school from 8:00 to 10:00 AM, and have a smaller amount of duty release time or coverage; or meet from 2:00 to 4:00 PM at the end of the day, with some coverage later in the afternoon. With dedicated time, members increase focus on learning and mentoring from one another and find it easier to attend. Often networks meet at a district office, especially if the district office is centrally located. However, if each school in the network takes turns to host meetings, members gain first-hand experience with the developing learning commons approach in each school, and it becomes easier to share student projects.

In most cases the teacher-librarian or teacher designated as lead learning commons teacher will attend network meetings. Perhaps not for all meetings but for some, consider that entire steering teams attend, or at least two members from the

Table 1.1 WSLLC Mentorship Approaches and Educator Actions

Mentorship Approaches:	Principal	Teacher-Librarian (TL)	*Other School Administrators	Teachers
COACHING	Coach faculty in preparing for, implementing and assessing WSLLC.	Coach teachers in collaborative planning, teaching, and assessing learning experiences.	Support the teachers/TL in coaching for co-teaching.	Open to coaching for collaborative practice; coach other team members in the process.
CONSULTING	Seek expertise within and beyond school to understand best WSLLC practice and resources.	Consult on curriculum, learning theory, instructional design, learning commons physical and virtual attributes.	Expertise on instructional leadership and design, specialty areas.	Expertise on students/grade/ subjects taught, methodology.
COLLABORATING	Expect, supervise, and evaluate ongoing co-planning, teaching, assessing across curriculum.	Initiate and implement ongoing co-planning, teaching, and assessing across curriculum.	Expect, support and model co-planned, taught, and assessed learning experiences in the learning commons.	Engage in and request co-planning, teaching, and assessing; determine best fit for current student need/area of study.
FACILITATION	Enable WSLLC teams to achieve their goals. Monitor and assess WSLLC. Initiate flexible scheduling.	Balance flexible schedules throughout year so all students and teachers share equitable WSLLC experiences on an ongoing, rotational basis.	Support/ design flexible timetables/ schedules; facilitate constructivist and collaborative learning and teaching throughout the school.	"Uncover" rather than "cover" curriculum—use constructivist, inquiry-based methodology for students to engage in deep thinking and learning experiences.

* Vice principal, department heads, etc.

team, to better support each other in sharing information and mentoring others upon return to their school sites, and to have dedicated time together to engage in learning and dialogue. District school library learning commons specialists often organize or facilitate networks of practice; if a district does not have such a specialist, the shared-leadership approach of teacher-librarians, lead learning commons teachers, principals, or steering teams taking turns hosting and organizing meetings among schools is a workable and worthwhile option. Provide mentorship at a broader level at network meetings by inviting guest experts to present and dialogue; if not available in person, some guest experts may agree to participate via technology.

Mentoring—coaching, consulting, collaborating, and facilitation—involves educators in various mentorship activities, advancing learning and teaching experiences throughout the school in the learning commons approach. Table 1.1 summarizes a variety of educator actions in the mentorship approaches.

Chapter 2

SELECTED MENTORING RESOURCES WITH STRATEGIES

Mentorship "supports the importance of job-embedded, relevant, point-of-need instruction for professional development ... include book studies, critical-friends groups, partnerships with universities ..." (Brown, Dotson, and Yontz, 2011, p. 57)

Mentors give and receive support locally through an assortment of study groups, partnerships, or activities—face to face or through technology such as social media—in which mentees openly discuss developing concepts, ideas, and challenges they face and strategies to try prior to implementing instructional approaches and coaching others. In this section, we will present ideas for strategies to use or adapt in mentoring, as well as a key recommended resource to support the strategy. Select other or additional resource(s) for using with the strategies as well.

WSLLC Mentorship Resource 1:

Teacher Librarian Learning Commons Collection (*Teacher Librarian: The Journal of School Library Professionals*, 2014)

WSLLC Mentorship Strategy 1:

Theory to Practice—How Others Develop WSLLC Mentoring

A great amount of the literature on school library to whole school learning commons transformation is appearing and growing in reflective, site- or district-based journal articles, blogs, wikis, papers, and other similar publication forums. This growing body of literature provides plenty of information and distance mentoring from other educators writing about different types of schools in a variety of locations, experiencing the processes, challenges, and successes on their journeys to the WSLLC. The online resource Teacher Librarian Learning Commons Collection provides readers with a broad selection of thirty articles originally published in *Teacher Librarian: The Journal of School Library Professionals* from 2010 to 2014 (Levitov and Kaaland, 2016). These articles relate to school library learning commons development, with new articles to be added on a timely basis as they appear in the subscribed journal. The articles range from the theoretical to the very practical, with most articles encompassing both, to varying degrees. Articles are often illustrated with photographs or other visuals. With the voices of fellow educators and experts in the field providing insight, encouragement, and ideas, schools can find situations similar to their own from this collection, or gain insight or next-step ideas from reading about a school context or grade level different than theirs. For example, a series of five articles by Christina A. Bentheim follows a middle school library to learning commons developmental journey throughout an entire school year, as media specialist and social studies instructional coach Bentheim reports on the "transition of her traditional middle school library into a learning commons for the 21st century." Realizing there wasn't a great amount of literature available at the time detailing such a transition as it occurred, with emphasis on the process over the outcome, Bentheim "recounts here her early plans and activities to transform the traditional library into a learning commons for the 21st century. Her ambition, ingenuity, and legwork paid off and her story offers both inspiration and concrete guidance and ideas for others" (*Teacher Librarian: The Journal of School Library Professionals*, 2014).

Have the steering team, or principal or teacher-librarian if a team has not yet been formed, read through the provided list of brief article annotations in the Teacher Librarian Learning Commons Collection and decide which articles or series seem most promising to coach thinking from schools with similar context, and consider articles ranging from an overall picture to a more detailed approach. Decide on a pertinent selection of articles and request that readers record responses individually and then collaboratively, using the three-column chart below. Have leadership or steering team members facilitate discussion of the responses, as well

Theory to Practice—How Others Develop WSLLC Mentoring

WSLLC ARTICLE TITLE:	ARTICLE AUTHOR(S):	ARTICLE SOURCE:
Theoretical Point(s) What theoretical point(s) do the writer(s) present? Who do they quote?	Application(s) How do the writer(s) apply the theoretical point(s)?	Adaptation(s) How do we use or adapt the application(s) in our WSLLC journey?

as gather responses to provide information for the next learning commons steps. Gather responses for this strategy or other strategies in this book online, using collaborative technology, and post on large poster paper in the school professional development area, ideally located within a physical and virtual space of the learning commons. Encourage principals, teacher-librarians, or steering teams to write their own article for this journal or other journals to add to the mentorship pool and growing WSLLC literature for other educators.

WSLLC Mentorship Resource 2:

Co-teaching and Collaboration: How and Why Two Heads Are Better Than One (Loertscher and Koechlin, 2015a)

WSLLC Mentorship Strategy 2:

Kindred Spirits—How Others Approach Co-Teaching and Collaboration

---

In addition to documenting school library to learning commons journeys, educators in many schools document and write about successful co-teaching events and strategies that present increasing knowledge on this critical learning commons process and provide further "distance mentoring." Many of the writers share their co-teaching experiences in articles that also appear in *Teacher Librarian* journal (Levitov and Kaaland, 2016). A selection of the articles focused on co-teaching and collaboration form the anthology *Co-teaching and Collaboration: How and Why Two Heads Are Better Than One* (Loertscher and Koechlin, 2015a). Discovering that another school, group, or educator has experiences similar or "kindred" to your own—in this case, implementing co-teaching—and examining what others say and do about it, is of great support and facilitates mentorship whether the team, group, or school is exploring or experienced in co-teaching and collaboration. Contributing writers in the anthology often share contact information for additional questions and discussion in benefit of their experience and wisdom.

This anthology works as a book study for a steering team, a teacher-librarian network group, or an entire faculty, if the faculty is preparing in background and shared vision for the learning commons approach and is ready to take or is taking the significant step of co-planning, teaching, and assessing learning experiences. If not used as a full book study, select one or two articles from the anthology to share and discuss with the principal, steering team, or entire faculty—although approaching the anthology as a book study and reading about a variety of similar and differing contexts provides broader insight and comparison. Divide the articles among members of the steering team, teacher-librarian group, or school faculty, and ask for each member to record similarities, differences, or applicable ideas garnered from the article(s) that they deem relevant to co-teaching and collaboration moving ahead in the school. Record thoughts on a master chart to facilitate future planning steps for co-planning, teaching, and assessing learning events and experiences. Post the chart in the school professional development physical and virtual spaces, such as the staff room or, ideally, the learning commons, or the teacher-librarian network group online space. As readers work through their article(s) or section of the anthology, request that they add comments to the chart and observe what others add to it as it grows. At a predetermined point, have readers reconvene and discuss the chart responses with teams, network group, or faculty, and vote on five key action ideas inspired by the study to move co-teaching and collaboration forward in their schools. To fuel a discussion about "kindred spirits" and collaboration, provide raspberry cordial, old-fashioned lemonade, coconut macaroons, tea biscuits, or shortbread to hearken back to the popular phrase from *Anne of Green Gables*. Use table 2.1 as a sample for the large posted or digital chart to summarize and build on thoughts and plans.

WSLLC Mentorship Resource 3:

Beyond Bird Units! Thinking and Understanding in Information-Rich and Technology-Rich Environments, Refresh Edition (Loertscher, Koechlin, and Zwaan, 2011a)

WSLLC Mentorship Strategy 3:

A Think Model a Week—Unlimited Tools for Mentoring Thinking in Co-Teaching

---

Educators mentoring others in the learning commons approach find that the think models in this resource foster collaborative planning, teaching, and assessing instruction. Recommended for kindergarten through grade 12, *Beyond Bird Units! Thinking and Understanding in Information-Rich and Technology-Rich Environments, Refresh Edition*, contains eighteen "think models" with concise steps as to how and why educators choose to use one model over another for a specific instructional purpose, along with ideas of possible curricular topics or themes suited to each model. For instance, "Model #8: Use the Decision Matrix" is well suited to the following purposes:

- Promote accurate data gathering
- Organize data for better decision making or understanding
- See the dangers of bad data in any cell
- Teach complex issues; solve complex problems

(Loertscher, Koechlin, and Zwaan, 2011a)

The "Decision Matrix" example model facilitates a strategy for co-teaching a learning event such as "comparing candidates for office" in government studies common across the grade levels.

The think models provide educators with unlimited tools for co-planning, teaching, and accessing a great range of curricular topics, themes, and outcomes. Have

Table 2.1 Kindred Spirits: Mentors in Co-teaching and Collaboration

Article Title: _____

Author(s): _____

School/Grades in Article: _____

Article Contact? _____

Similarities between school in article and our school	Differences between school in article and our school	Ideas for our school to explore/implement

teacher-librarians, or other instructional leaders facilitating the strategy, introduce a think model a week at staff, department, or team meetings, to provide teachers with insight into the models, curricular connections, and time to process thoughts about how and where to use particular think models in practice and mentoring co-teaching. Share models used in co-taught learning experiences, highlighting the particular model when sharing the learning experience. Discuss job-embedded examples and pose questions to increase comfort with moving into using, building upon, and creating more think models as part of co-planning, teaching, and assessing learning experiences through collaborative practice.

WSLLC Mentorship Resource 4:

"Imagine the Possibilities" (Lunny and Sullivan, 2014)

WSLLC Mentorship Strategy 4:

Animating WSLLC—Teacher-Librarian as Instructional Mentor

Educators unfamiliar with the instructional mentorship of working with a teacher-librarian on the faculty—for a variety of reasons, as pointed out in the first chapter of this book—leave teachers and administrators in many schools without the experience of co-planning, teaching, and assessing instruction with a teacher-librarian. "Imagine the Possibilities" is a brief animated presentation that highlights transitions from school library to learning commons, and delineates major aspects of the role of effective teacher-librarian leadership. The animated resource highlights three major areas teacher-librarians lead and mentor in: literacy, technology, and instructional design. Each of these areas is further showcased with sub-headings pertaining to them, such as "transliteracy," "digital citizenship," "personalization of learning," and more (Lunny and Sullivan, 2014). The creators of the presentation find a unique way to inform fellow educators about teacher-librarian leadership possibilities in the learning commons—and, most importantly, the impact such possibilities have on student learning through teacher and teacher-librarian collaboration.

Share the video with teacher-librarian network groups, as well as in schools with the principal or steering team in preparation to view it with the broader faculty and facilitate conversation relating to pedagogical leadership in the WSLLC. Have the steering team model from the video presentation and create their own more local representation of the teacher-librarian or lead learning commons teacher leadership theme, keeping the leadership attributes from the resource—literacy, technology, and instructional design. Have the steering team use animation tools as in the model, or decide on their own form of representation, such as co-creating a collage, poster, Animoto, a combination of representation forms … even a short live skit highlighting the teacher-librarian leadership possibility areas. Discuss and add to the sub-headings shown in the three major leadership areas based on what is contextually important to student learning at the school and the development of co-teaching plans to further them. Use the following chart to record possibilities.

Animating WSLLC—Teacher-Librarian as Instructional Mentor

LITERACY	TECHNOLOGY	INSTRUCTIONAL DESIGN	WSLLC TEACHER and TEACHER-LIBRARIAN POSSIBILITIES
Sub-Headings	Sub-Headings	Sub-Headings	Collaboration Ideas
Reading	*Digital citizenship*	*Personalization of learning*	
Transliteracy	*Web safety*	*?*	
?	*?*	*?*	
?	?	?	
?	?	?	

> **WSLLC Mentorship Resource 5:**
>
> *School Libraries in Canada* (Grose, 2016)
>
> **WSLLC Mentorship Strategy 5:**
>
> Curriculum Corners—Teachers Mentor Teachers

Curricular mentorship, support, and teaming is invaluable for new or experienced teachers as they strive to match ever-changing and expanding curricular mandates, teaching methods, and expectations with daily student needs and outcomes so that all students experience learning success. Mentorship among educators in a collaborative approach facilitates staying current in curricular changes and teaching methodology, both topical and pedagogical, along with co-determined student needs. Instructional leaders in the school—the principal, other administrators, and specialists such as the teacher-librarian and department heads—approach curricular mentorship in a variety of ways dependent upon the situation at hand: facilitating, coaching, consulting, and especially collaborating through co-teaching to bring the curriculum to life. The online journal *School Libraries in Canada*—accessible at no cost, as it is sponsored by the Canadian Voices for School Libraries (CVSL)—focuses considerable portions of its current and archived issues on school library learning commons developments and resources, as well as curricular topics or teaching and learning processes pertinent to schools not only in Canada but around the world. Recent issues contain broad curricular topics with implementation strategies, articles, and recommended resources on a range of subjects such as politics, law, food and nutrition, science and technology, history, business, fitness, the arts, and others. Readers of *School Libraries in Canada* adapt topics or themes to suit their local context and grade levels. For example, the issue on politics includes an article on how to involve students in an upcoming Canadian election, applicable to other elections or similar to articles in the United States or other countries on student involvement in elections. Schools use the implementation strategy ideas and many of the articles or resources, such as picture books or novels, as applicable to subject and context.

Teacher-librarians and instructional leaders can use this journal or similar resources by choosing a new or standard curricular area teachers are working on and mentoring professional practice through collaborative planning, teaching, and assessing of an interdisciplinary approach. Invite varied teacher expertise to "corners of the table" to co-plan interdisciplinary learning experiences such as projects or quests. For example, if implementing a new social studies curriculum, invite the social studies teacher, English or language arts teacher, math teacher, and drama teacher "to the table" to plan an interdisciplinary study for the students combining student skills, outcomes, and processes common to each subject or discipline area. What literature study or novel brings the social studies outcomes to life? What common writing and communication expectations do the teachers have? How do students express their learning in numbers as well as words? Does the drama class engage in student improvisations based on the outcome? Might "the table" have more corners and include more teachers? What rubrics can the teachers co-develop together with the students? How do the teacher planning teams ensure that all student needs will be included in the project or study? Use the sample shown in table 2.2, with four corners, to facilitate planning.

WSLLC Mentorship Resource 6:

"Collaborative Teaching Recording Template" (in "Assessing Effective School Library Learning Commons Themes," Brown and Sykes, 2016, p. 23)

WSLLC Mentorship Strategy 6:

Keeping Track—Document Co-Teaching Plans for Reflection and Reference

---

As educators become comfortable with mentoring through collaboration and co-teaching, they repeat and adapt successful learning experiences and plan new ones. Keeping records of learning events facilitates planning and keeps planning teams on track, providing "evidence of a thoughtful and planned approach to the learning events that occur in the physical and virtual SLLC based on curricular mandate and analysis of student learning data" (Brown and Sykes, 2016, p. 19). Teacher-librarians or lead learning commons teachers and other instructional leaders cumulate records of their work in collaborative planned, taught, and assessed learning events over many different curricular levels, subjects, and outcomes, to draw upon for continued use or adaptation as well as for increased information for curricular and student need choices in developing print and digital resource collections. Student and teacher feedback, reflections, evaluations, and recommendations of the learning experience in archived records inform future planning of the

Table 2.2 WSLLC Curriculum Corners

Corner 1 Subject Area: Curricular Outcome:	CROSS-CURRICULAR STRATEGIES ↓	Corner 3 Subject Area: Curricular Outcome:
Corner 2 Subject Area: Curricular Outcome:		Corner 4 Subject Area: Curricular Outcome:

same or similar learning experiences. These insights make for valuable discussion regarding student assessment results in areas taught through collaboration, via professional development possibilities, in teacher-librarian network group discussions or mentoring situations, or by sharing in journal articles or other venues. Use the template on the following page for keeping track of the various planning activities and roles and responsibilities inherent in the process. Adapt the template to local needs or circumstances as required.

WSLLC Mentorship Resource 7:

"Exciting Times—A Transformation of Media Centers, Media Specialists, and Learning: A District's Philosophy" (Sobolik, Russell, Klatt, Thompson, Jones, and Wieczorek, 2014)

WSLLC Mentorship Strategy 7:

Continuous Commons Breakfast Club—Feeder School Mentoring

Whether the school library to learning commons transformation is developing in a primary, elementary, middle, junior high, or senior high school, it benefits students greatly if learning experiences, expectations, spaces, and places provide a consistent approach along the way, as many students move from K–12 in the same general vicinity or district. Educators in schools in the same community mentor each other so that students benefit from similar expectations and rich, innovative learning environments. As seen in chapter four in this book, national or state polices and standards exist for purposes of developing common expectations in learning environments such as school libraries, and work toward equity in accessibility and learning experiences. Many school districts strive to implement these standards and policies to unite their schools in provision of equitable school libraries to learning commons experiences and services. The resource in this strategy relates the documentation of three schools in the Kettle Moraine School District in southeast Wisconsin as an example of a school district's philosophy and actions in changing library media and technology support across schools for the personalization of student learning. The three schools in the article—an elementary, middle, and high school—share their work and progress to date. Each school notes, "Changing the role of the media specialist is an essential step in transforming a school media center into a learning commons."

Whether your school district is collectively transforming school libraries to learning commons and correspondingly adjusting the role of the teacher-librarian or not, schools create synergy and continuity within their local communities by developing feeder school teams to mentor each other and plan articulation between schools in learning commons approach growth and development. It can be useful for schools to consider applying for grant funding for development or research, to move forward together in transforming their libraries. To

Collaborative Teaching Recording Template

Topic: _____

Subject Area(s): _____

Courses: _____

Teacher(s): _____

Grade: _____

1. What do we want the students **to know** when they have finished the learning event?
   (Learning Objectives/Outcomes/Curriculum Content)

2. What do we want the **final project or culminating activity** to look like?
   (Form, format, media, etc.)   How will we assess it?

3. What **skills** and **processes** do the students need to practice to be successful in this learning event?
   Independent Learning Skills/Processes
   Problem-Solving Skills/Processes
   Content-Specific Skills/Processes

4. What **resources** do we need for the students to be successful?
   Print   Digital   Human   Community

5. What **roles** do the teacher(s) have?

6. What **roles** do the teacher-librarian, learning commons lead teacher, other library staff, educators or specialists have?

7. Schedule / **Time Frame** for activities

8. **Assessment / Evaluation:** What teacher-made **rubrics** do we use? What student-developed **rubrics** do we accept?

9. **Review and Recycle**
   What parts of the learning event need to be adjusted for the next class?
   What resources need to be acquired to do this learning event again?
   What skills and processes have the students mastered?
   Who will **write** this learning event up for publication?

T.E.A.M. = Together each achieves more

Source: Brown and Sykes, 2016, p. 23. Reprinted with permission.

create such a "continuous commons" in the community, someone has to open the doors between schools—usually one of the principals, teacher librarians, or members of the steering team—and invite their counterparts from the feeder schools to meet to discuss the evolving learning commons approach in each school. It can be challenging to find time to meet and plan within schools, never mind between schools; yet the continuous experience, mentoring, and support that happens, to benefit the students and teachers, is well worth the effort. Form a "breakfast club," where steering teams or representatives from the schools meet on the way to work, perhaps at a nearby café or coffee shop, or in the school cafeteria or learning commons in one of the group of schools. Breakfast meetings are productive and enjoyable, as participants pause on their way to demanding days.

Initiate discussion in preliminary cross-school breakfast or other meetings, with representatives or steering teams from each school sharing and discussing articles mentioned in this strategy or others like it. At the onset, have each school complete a succinct checklist or survey that addresses similar components in the progress of students from elementary to high school in a learning commons approach, to determine where mentorship needs and common areas for collaboration exist. For example, develop common writing and reference guides that begin in primary school with citations—citing titles, authors, and dates—and builds to working with a style guide on the virtual learning commons in a senior high school. Find out whether basic learning commons items such as furniture, books, or other resources are given a bulk discount if shared between a number of schools. Engage educators across schools in co-planned, taught, and assessed literacy projects such as involving students in planning and holding a community literary festival with authors K-12 appearing in person or using video conferencing. Display, view, share, and perform student projects across grades and schools. Use the checklist provided in table 2.3 to initiate discussion of common matters and ideas between feeder schools.

WSLLC Mentorship Resource 8:
"Teacher Librarians: Mavens in a Digital Age" (Webb and Ray, 2015)

WSLLC Mentorship Strategy 8:
Techsperts—Technology Mentors

Traditional perceptions and stereotypes prevail around the word "librarian," yet librarians and teacher-librarians today provide expertise and leadership in technology, particularly technology for learning. Vancouver (Washington) Public Schools recognizes this and invests in teacher-librarians to serve as digital mentors and district leaders. Although we hear of many school districts reducing teacher-librarian positions, this Washington school district was "fortunate to be able to retain and empower its teacher librarians by expanding the scope of their roles, and we strongly believe other districts can benefit from this model. Teacher librarians

Table 2.3 Continuous Commons Checklist

SCHOOL NAME:_____

GRADES: _____

STUDENT LEARNING	PHYSICAL WSLLC	VIRTUAL WSLLC
☐ Multi-literacy	☐ Designed for learning needs of students	☐ Designed for learning needs of students
☐ Inquiry-based		
☐ Project-based	☐ Flexibly scheduled	☐ Continually monitored and updated
☐ Problem-based	☐ Group areas	
☐ Experiential (play, makerspaces, arts)	☐ Individual study/reading areas	☐ Knowledge-building centers
☐ Cooperative learning	☐ Welcoming, safe, bright, spacious, comfortable	☐ Variety of learning activities
☐ Critical thinking	☐ Knowledge-production areas; e.g., high-tech makerspaces; digital creating/editing	☐ Gateway to digital resources and libraries
☐ Personalized		
☐ Participatory		
☐ Knowledge-building, creating, sharing	☐ Collaborative community space; e.g., "coffee house"	☐ Active learning in real time; e.g., social networking, gaming, webinars, blogs, videoconference
☐ Access to library professionals and co-teaching	☐ Space where students share information, story tell, dramatize	
☐ Inclusive learning resources	☐ Current collections based on student outcomes/needs	☐ Student reference/ handbook guide used by all teachers
☐ Develop lifelong readers	☐ Shelves on walls or in pods on wheels	
☐ Variety of learning activities		
☐ Accommodate all learning modalities	☐ Display areas, smart boards showcase a continually changing variety of student work; e.g., art, videos, etc.	☐
☐		☐
☐		☐
☐	☐	
	☐	
	☐	

are ideally suited to lead, teach and support students and teachers in 21st-century schools" (Webb and Ray, 2015). To involve the district's teacher-librarians or "digital mavens" as digital mentors, the district initially implemented a plan for its thirty-three teacher-librarians to train teachers in using a new on-demand video service. Following this project's success, the role of teacher-librarians in the district was expanded to deliver instructional technology support, working closely with curriculum and instructional technology teams at the district level and in a variety of mentoring approaches in the schools, mentoring teachers, students, and also parents in a systematic way, "promoting the safe, effective and responsible use of digital tools and resources" (Webb and Ray, 2015).

Teacher-librarians and many learning commons lead teachers demonstrate proficiency as some of the most technology-savvy educational professionals—and, along with their expertise in leading learning and instruction, these "cybrarians" bring co-teaching into the virtual learning commons. Table 2.4 focuses discussion on digital mentorship needs in a school, listing some examples of common digital needs. Use this table to brainstorm where mentoring is most needed, based on your student data and context.

Table 2.4   WSLLC Techspert Mentoring

DIGITAL NEED	MENTORING STRATEGY
Creating knowledge-building centers on the Virtual Learning Commons (VLC)	• Use the learning commons website, Knowledge Building Centers page (Loertscher and Koechlin, 2016),with the WSLLC steering team to support and create plans to mentor teachers for co-teaching and collaboration in the VLC
Increase e-book interactive dialogue	• Examine design of VLC student e-book clubs, response blogs, and work with students to develop interactive e-book dialogue platforms (students mentor students)
Integrate high-tech makerspaces into co-taught learning experiences	• Visit other schools to view and understand makerspaces (teacher mentor other teachers or teacher-librarians)
Examine student data to best infuse technology for learning	• Cooperative analysis of student data; principal mentors faculty • Presentation highlighting examples of possible technology supports for students (teacher-librarian mentors faculty)
Support students becoming good digital citizens through social media	• Incorporate social media design into co-taught learning events (teacher-librarian mentors teachers)
Develop online communities of practice	• Decide components of community of practice (school specialists/administrators mentor teachers) • Co-design and engage participants in community of practice (teacher-librarian mentors teachers)

> **WSLLC Mentorship Resource 9:**
>
> "Mentorship of New Teacher-Librarians" (Buckley and Arruda, 2014)
>
> **WSLLC Mentorship Strategy 9:**
>
> Mentors as Superheroes! Reflective Writing and Comic Strip

The conference presentation "Mentorship of New Teacher-Librarians" provides advice, information, and additional references for administrators and library leaders, for mentoring new teacher-librarians or learning commons lead teachers for success. The authors share research in the area of mentoring new teacher-librarians, their experiences, and common new teacher-librarian needs and strategies for mentors to be aware of and consider. As in other educational specialties, the move from classroom teacher to whole school library learning commons specialist is overwhelming at times, and in most cases the teacher-librarian or appointed learning commons lead teacher is the only one to hold that position within a school. The authors summarize and detail predominant mentorship needs of beginning teacher-librarians, including the notions of support for the library role, not reinventing the wheel since much is available from others, beginning with a few key resources, learning how to prioritize actions in this new role to avoid feeling overwhelmed, being part of a professional network, and having technology support. Several different models exist for new teacher-librarian mentorship; the authors highlight a model proposed from a study on beginning teacher mentorship in which

- the centre of the relationship is focused on learning (student learning and new-teacher learning) and
- there are multiple mentors (none are "assigned") and
- no individualized (formal) plan, instead
- a focus on intellectual interaction

(Hellsten, Prytula, Ebanks, and Lai, 2009)

The authors state that multiple mentors provide support through activities such as regular meetings with principals and district library consultants, attending in-service sessions if available for new teacher-librarians as well as attending ongoing professional events and programs, joining teacher-librarian associations, networks, or official mentorship programs, twinning schools or attending family of schools meetings (as mentioned in strategy 7 in this chapter), and participating in a variety of communication strategies and forums (Buckley and Arruda, 2014).

Each member of a steering team or teacher-librarian network group engages in mentoring or being mentored as they work to move forward with the learning commons approach. Engage steering team or network group members in reflective writing to think deeply about a mentor who is like a "superhero" to them, impacting their career or learning, focusing on the areas of school library and learning commons. Following privately writing about how and why their mentor impacted them, request that each participant draw a one- to four-panel comic strip demonstrating why and how this mentor is a "superhero" for him or her. The comic strips can range from stick figures to caricature, depending on how simple or detailed the participant wishes to make them. Share the comic strips, with the identity of the mentor remaining anonymous unless the participant wants to share with the team or group—and, if needed, has permission to share, especially if they wish to post the "superhero mentor" comic strips in the physical or virtual learning commons professional area.

WSLLC Mentorship Resource 10:

Conferences and Meetings (American Association of School Librarians [AASL], 2016a)

WSLLC Mentorship Strategy 10:

Attend a Conference!

School library learning commons pioneers and experts whose resources appear throughout this book mentor principals, teachers, and teacher-librarians. Though most of us cannot access experts on demand, their publications, websites, courses, and conference presentations assist educators in mentoring school library to learning commons initiatives. Organizations such as the American Association of School Librarians (AASL) or the International Association of School Librarianship (IASL) offer regular conferences relating to school libraries and learning commons developments. Although many conferences and professional learning events are available locally or through technology, attending a conference in another state, province, territory, or country provides a great learning and networking experience, allowing educators to meet colleagues or experts in the field that they may have only encountered previously online. Attending such professional learning events with a colleague from the district or another faculty member is beneficial, as both parties support each other in sharing or implementing new ideas upon returning to their school or district. Conference information is posted regularly on organization websites; many school districts and teacher associations provide partial to full funding for attending conferences near and far. Applying to present at a conference and mentoring others through sharing your own WSLLC experiences is additionally professionally enriching.

Chapter 3

MENTORING CASE STUDIES

The possibilities are endless when school district administrators and library media specialists work together.... As a result, students will be better prepared for what awaits them in this challenging yet exciting world. (Sobolik, Russell, Klatt, Thompson, Jones, and Wieczorek, 2014, p. 25)

Case studies facilitate reflection and comparison to a practitioner's own context. The following five case studies relate a variety of the WSLLC development scenarios as supported through mentoring, from elementary through high school levels. The case studies depict experiences in a number of different situations over time, to showcase possible approaches. Share with a mentee, the steering team members, or the broader faculty to begin or continue discussion on the learning commons approach. Each case study is followed by discussion questions to open and guide conversation.

Case Study 1:
Teacher-librarian mentoring principal, teachers, other library staff, WSLLC team[*]

"Shannon" is very excited to be hired as the teacher-librarian/learning commons lead teacher of a large urban school of over 600 students ranging from kindergarten to ninth grade. Students from grades five through nine learn through second-language immersion. Although the school has not had a teacher-librarian for some

[*]Based on a compilation of experience, courtesy of Erin Hansen, School Library Learning Commons Specialist, Alberta.

time, the principal fully supports the specialty and the creating of a school library to learning commons vision. Yet at the same time Shannon begins with little time dedicated to lead the development, as she is "wearing many hats," including teaching middle school classes. Shannon receives technical support from a library assistant 25 hours per week, as well as lunch supervisors four days a week for 30 minutes. The school district provides central technology support two days per week, which means Shannon concentrates more on mentoring teachers to use technology for learning in collaborative planning and less on "fixing" technology infrastructure issues.

Where to begin? Shannon decides to implement "quick wins" as she tackles the tougher challenges of transforming the school library into a learning commons. The principal encourages the faculty to access Shannon's services into planning learning commons experiences and events, provides funding for new resources, and plans for changes to the physical commons. The principal helps Shannon put together a steering team comprising the principal, the teacher-librarian, the library technician, and four other teachers—one from each division and the music specialist. The principal invites Shannon as a special guest presenter to a parent council meeting to share the vision and get support from the school parent leadership team. Shannon also starts a student learning commons club to develop a student vision, and a parent volunteer program to involve parents in the developments.

The physical learning commons in Shannon's new position was built more than fifty years ago, when the school was built, so Shannon notices limitations to space, an awkward shape, crowded work areas, and unmovable shelves. She also notices numerous large bright windows, a great assortment of tables, and many computers—laptops, laptop carts, iPads, iPods—that operate through a wireless hub. Statistics show high book circulation rates, and Shannon observes a great deal of eagerness of students to come to the physical space, along with long line-ups and busy staff. She immediately adds two "kid-powered" self-checkouts salvaged from old desktop computers. She shifts the vision of book exchange to move away from scheduled to flexible visits. Shannon then rearranges existing furnishings to create multi-purpose spaces for reading/listening/viewing/creating. She notices high computer use in the physical commons but no spare computers for individual resource searchers. Again she salvages—this time two older notebook computers, to be dedicated to searchers. Shannon creates student work showcases throughout the space to highlight curricular projects.

Although it is tempting to begin and continue with making physical changes, Shannon knows that they must begin the school library to learning commons transformation with the pedagogical approach, to focus on school learning goals and outcomes. She continues with designing the space to meet the needs of the students. Taking a deep breath a few weeks later, Shannon introduces the pedagogical approach at a faculty meeting, sharing the government-mandated learning commons policy, technology framework, and *Leading Learning: Standards of Practice for School Library Learning Commons in Canada* (Canadian Library Association, 2014b). She mentions that the 2014 Canadian Library Association president considered the learning commons standard publication as a "definitive learning support that is critical for all Canadian schools" (Voices for School Libraries Network,

2016), and that the key to developing the approach is to "Ensure all members of the learning community are part of SLLC development—create an SLLC team to lead, implement, and sustain the effort" (Sykes, 2014, p. 10).

The steering team proceed to use the five standards as a starting point for planning and focused discussions, noting that "Implementing and sustaining *Leading Learning: Standards of Practice for School Library Learning Commons in Canada* will require each school to pose many questions and collaborate for strategic solutions to move through and beyond its phases…. By following the steps to implementation and using strategic tools to provide direction and sustenance, students will receive the best possible preparation for their future" (Sykes, 2014, pp. 11, 12). The steering team creates and administers a staff and student survey, seeking information on current likes or dislikes, and wishes and dreams for the space and the approach.

Shannon shares the brief and catchy animation "Imagine the Possibilities" (Lunny and Sullivan, 2014), which highlights the learning commons approach and the changing role of the teacher-librarian in co-teaching. Shannon extends the invitation to collaborate on curriculum with her. The fifth grade team steps up to the plate with a language co-teaching project aimed at creating a French and English recipe collaboration and accompanying video. Four classes work with the teaching team and invite parents to a concluding celebration. The students present their project to other students in the same grade and different grades.

Shannon realizes how empowering her role is—as well as limiting, in how much she can do in the time she has. She sets priorities and thinks about mentoring the learning commons approach with the following goals in mind:

- Weed the physical collection – teacher, library staff mentoring
- Organize the "back room" – inventory – library staff mentoring
- Organize a PD day for teachers – online resources – teacher mentoring
- Examine the digital collection – overlaps? – teacher, library staff mentoring
- Look for co-teaching partners – teacher mentoring
- Look for community partners (e.g., public library) – engage community
- Set up a Virtual Learning Commons – teacher, library staff mentoring

With the mind of a researcher, Shannon knows that her next steps involve needing to know what is working, what isn't, what to do next, and what insights or mentoring did others offer to her and the school.

Case Study 1 Discussion Questions

1. What advice do you give to Shannon for next steps?
2. Who might Shannon mentor or be mentored by in her next steps?
3. What key resources does Shannon employ? Do you have others you use in similar situations?
4. How do members of the steering team mentor and support Shannon in the next steps?

Case Study 2:
Principal mentoring teacher-librarian/learning commons lead teacher, WSLLC team[*]

Samuel is the new principal at a very small elementary school with about 200 students and 8 teachers. When first built, the school population thrived, but as the school and neighborhood aged, enrollment declined. The school building is beautiful—especially the library, with its enormous windows and solid oak shelves. There is very little seating among the rows of books, however, and it seems that student activity involves classes coming in to sign out books en masse at dedicated times. This activity contrasts sharply with the school Samuel left behind, where the library is a hub of activity transitioning into a learning commons. Samuel was the vice principal, and he worked closely with a teacher-librarian, other school special-ists, and most of the teachers, to bring his expertise in technology to the learning commons team. He was involved in designing instruction for learning experiences in the increasingly flexible physical and virtual spaces, and despite his busy sched-ule, was able to participate in co-teaching a number of learning projects. He was able to guide teacher planning teams using student data so that learning would be personalized, and he worked directly with many students to better understand their learning needs through co-taught learning events and experiences across the grades and curriculum. He mentored teachers, coaching and supporting them as he and the teacher-librarian introduced innovation in teaching methods and new and evolving technology. He created a "student tech team" so that students could help other students and teachers with various tech needs. Individual students vis-ited the physical school library learning commons independently to sign out books or receive reference help as needed, supported by the library technician as required.

Now as principal, Samuel hopes to mentor the library to learning commons approach in his new school. As the school population is small, he does not have other administrators or specialists on faculty. But he does have an enthusiastic library technician, interested teachers, and excited students and parents keen to develop the school library into learning commons approach. Despite his even busier new schedule, Samuel schedules time to form and meet with a WSLLC steering team. Two teachers volunteer to join the team, along with the library technician. One of the teachers is particularly interested in seeing the library transform into a vibrant learning commons in both physical and virtual spaces. Samuel is able to mentor her as learning commons lead teacher, based on his knowledge from his former school. He also is delighted that the teacher-librarian from his for-mer school agrees to mentor this teacher as well. The learning commons lead teacher at Samuel's new school starts spending many lunch and after-school hours in the school library, working with a student library club and parent volunteers to move shelves, salvage tables and chairs, and create spaces for the students to work together or independently in and areas to display their work. She begins the process of updating and weeding out the collection, with the experienced teacher-librarian

---

[*]Based on a compilation of the author's experience.

or Samuel coaching her in this process a few times a month. However, Samuel worries about the most important thing: providing time in the learning commons for the pedagogical aspects of the approach—co-teaching, planning, and assessing learning events—as there is no flexible time in staffing allocations in this small school. Samuel decides to teach a favorite subject—language arts—to the learning commons lead teacher's class for two hours a day, with the expectation that she will collaborate with the other teachers in co-planning and teaching a project each month with a different teacher, hoping to involve all of the students and teachers in such a learning experience over the year. If an emergent event requires Samuel's attention, the learning commons lead teacher returns to her class, and the co-teacher in the learning commons continues until Samuel returns.

Samuel works with all of the teachers in analyzing student learning data. They discover a disparity in reading success, both in the content area and for enjoyment, which Samuel knows the learning commons approach impacts. He shares a summary of student impact research that the teachers were not previously familiar with. The steering team successfully applies for a grant for a wide variety of reading material that they select to engage and inspire the students based on authoritative children's literature criteria; the teacher-librarian from Samuel's previous school mentors the team in the use of these criteria for resource selection. The parent-teacher association raises funds for a mobile iPad lab. The teacher-librarian mentor from Samuel's previous school also reminds Samuel about the online reference center provided by the government, which gives free access to a wide range of e-books, reference materials, and assistive technology. This mentor also co-plans a professional day about the online reference center with Samuel's learning commons lead teacher. The learning commons lead teacher begins to create a virtual learning commons with "rooms" for all classes to post, collaborate, and create in.

In the two co-teaching hours of the day, the physical learning commons is busy with a variety of burgeoning student projects that range from creating video book talks for posting on the virtual commons, to building accurately scaled dioramas of endangered species habitats in a math and science project. Most teachers embrace the approach, and the learning commons lead teacher approaches teachers hesitant about co-planning and teaching, to plan smaller events such as mini-lessons on accessing e-books or a brief writing project introducing the iPads. The library technician is freer to support individual students and teachers, and is pleased that the students are signing out books independently and increasing their independent learning skills and processes in co-taught learning experiences. She focuses on helping students choose reading materials or helping them with project questions.

Over the course of the year Samuel works with the teachers to review regular formative and summative assessments of student work and examine student report card results—and at the end of the year they review the statewide test results. Although the learning community is seeing changes in regular assessment results, they delight to see overall state test reading scores increase too. The learning commons lead teacher takes a sabbatical to certify as a teacher-librarian, and one of the other teachers approaches Samuel about stepping into her role while she is gone. Samuel teaches one of his subjects a couple hours a day. The interim learning commons lead teacher serves on the steering team and is eager to continue implementing the approach, having learned a great deal from the previous teacher. Samuel is delighted and looks forward to further expanding the learning commons transformation through effective mentoring in the coming year.

Case Study 2 Discussion Questions

1. Discuss the pros and cons of Samuel's approach.
2. What mentorship strategies could Samuel use with the new learning commons lead teacher?
3. Would Samuel's approach work in your school? Why or why not? What do you do differently or complementarily within your context?

Case Study 3:
Principal mentoring other principals[*]

Tamara is the principal of a large urban high school with over 2,000 students. The school takes pride in its library, which has grown and changed in many ways over time—especially over the past few years, as the whole school focused on a school library to learning commons approach. The high school teacher-librarian follows and shares the transformational work performed by other high schools to transform their school libraries, through articles in journals such as *Teacher Librarian* (Levitov and Kaaland, 2016), blogs such as "The Unquiet Librarian" (Hamilton, 2015), conferences such as Treasure Mountain Research Retreat (Loertscher, 2015c), and books such as *The New Learning Commons: Where Learners Win! Reinventing School Libraries and Computer Labs, 2nd Ed.* (Loertscher, Koelchin, and Zwaan, 2011b). One particular article that Tamara and the teacher-librarian share with the faculty focuses on a high school building similar to theirs but with fewer students (Cicchetti, 2010). That library, like theirs, had been at times "dedicated to books"; Tamara gives her full support to the teacher-librarian to form a WSLLC team and transform the environment dedicated to "a model where student learning comes first."

Any day that Tamara steps into the learning commons, she sees a dynamic center of student learning activity. The teacher-librarian is usually working with one or two other teachers and their classes, co-teaching a curricular event. Groups of students work together or independently, reading, discussing, computing, creating, researching, and applying findings to their learning. Tamara is delighted that student achievement scores rise, and student satisfaction surveys relating to the learning commons transition prove very positive. However, during a WSLLC steering team meeting, the teacher-librarian mentions that many of the students coming into high school seem unfamiliar with using and learning in a school library learning commons. Her colleagues in the feeder junior high school and elementary schools also notice and acknowledge this as the students move from one campus

---

[*]Based on a compilation of the author's experience.

to another. As the discussion continues, they wonder how consistent the learning commons approach is across schools, especially using instructional design focused on student learning data to co-teach. They wonder how to increase consistency in the approach as students move along grade divisions. Some of the feeder schools begin to explore transitioning from school library to learning commons; others fully develop the process of implementation of the approach. The teacher-librarian seeks Tamara's advice for her and her colleagues to advance consistency across the schools.

Tamara thinks about this issue, noting to address it at the next regular community feeder school principal meeting, which occurs a few times a year mostly to coordinate calendars or plan transitions between grades. At the next meeting, Tamara talks about the issue of WSLLC consistency between feeder schools. She wonders where the feeder schools align in the process and makes a case for a consistent approach, mentioning the research behind the learning commons approach and the results the high school is experiencing. The other principals show a great deal of interest in the description and the student impact results Tamara cites for their shared student demographic. Yet most of them wonder how to get the whole school involved, especially in co-teaching. Others wonder about the expense of designing a new school library. Tamara assures them that the learning commons approach isn't only about designing a new school library, although enriched learning environments do develop over time, with outcomes-based budgets and community effort. The most important thing is the collaboration around instructional design that happens between teachers and the teacher-librarian, based on student learning data. The other principals comment that most of their schools do not have a teacher-librarian, due to budget constraints, although the junior high school employs a part-time teacher-librarian. Tamara tells them that in the professional resources her teacher-librarian shares, there are many cases where schools form WSLLC steering teams—and if they do not have a teacher-librarian, they likely do have a teacher who is interested in leading the learning commons effort. This teacher is usually someone who has expressed interest in and demonstrated propensity for instructional leadership, technology, and literacy.

Tamara shares an idea that the other principals favor. She asks them each to identify such a teacher at their schools, and with the mentorship of Tamara, the other principals, and Tamara's teacher-librarian, as well as some shared professional development time and activities, they create a feeder school learning commons community of practice. The teacher-librarians and lead learning commons teachers meet physically and virtually to collaborate on creating a consistent approach throughout the community of schools. They bring back to their schools what they learn from the community of practice, to ignite and inform a consistent approach. With mentorship from the high school and each other over time, the feeder school community of practice shares information about the approach within each school, and each forms its own steering team. The community of practice provides a place for mentoring teacher-librarians or lead learning commons teachers new to the group, so efforts in developing consistency continue when original members move on. Tamara's teacher-librarian is enthused about providing mentorship in the community of practice, as well as about learning how the learning commons approach develops and grows from kindergarten through high school.

Case Study 3 Discussion Questions

1. Has your school considered the lens of a feeder school community of practice? What benefits can occur? What barriers do you see in the way?
2. Thinking about barriers, what ideas might overcome them?
3. Do you think Tamara's community of practice will thrive once Tamara has moved on? Why or why not?

Case Study 4:
School district teacher-librarian
mentoring district schools[*]

Lauren is nervously anticipating her first school district WSLLC community of practice meeting as the new district teacher-librarian. The district, comprising twenty schools spread across several small towns and villages, is at a variety of phases in the school library to learning commons transformation. Lauren had previously led school library transformation initiatives in an elementary school in a nearby city, and had begun school library to learning commons transformation in one of the three high schools in her current district prior to her maternity leave. Lauren had wished to return to work part-time, and serendipitously the school district offered her a part-time position as learning commons consultant to lead a community of practice through concerns, questions, and moving toward the innovative approach.

Lauren is excited about the challenges and possibilities of her new position. She thinks about ways of approaching the creation of a community of practice in the district through mentoring processes—coaching where most needed or applicable, and collaborating, consulting, or facilitating elsewhere to be able to mentor the schools in the pedagogy. Although her position is part-time, Lauren knows that each school in the district is at different phases in learning commons development, and once she captures a picture of the district school library to learning commons continuum, she will be able to create reasonable and achievable methods of mentoring suited to the varying contexts.

Lauren requests that the schools each send their principal and teacher-librarian—or select or appoint a learning commons lead teacher if they don't have a teacher-librarian—to attend the first meeting, arranging coverage to release practitioners from duties an hour earlier. If possible, Lauren requests that other members of the school library staff or steering team, if one is already formed, also attend. Lauren holds the community of practice meeting at her former high school, who are delighted to host. Lauren asks the other schools to volunteer to host future community of practice meetings. She learns where each of her schools believe

---

[*]Based on a compilation of the author's experience.

themselves to be on a learning commons continuum, using the themes and indicators from *Leading Learning: Standards of Practice for School Library Learning Commons in Canada* (Canadian Library Association, 2014b). This resource provides Lauren with a common source to provide continuity in the approach and track growth. She shares the definition of a learning commons from the resource and guides the school representatives through the themes and indicators, encouraging them to assess where they think they fit in each theme. The meeting is a great success, with most of the schools represented; Lauren is able to visit a few of the schools not in attendance and gather information at their sites. Lauren thus develops a good picture of where the schools in the district practice with the approach, and she decides how and where to extend her efforts.

Over time Lauren discovers that some schools, like her former high school, move along very quickly with the approach. Lauren is still able to mentor the new teacher-librarian who took her place through occasional visits, phone calls, and e-mail. Other schools require more of Lauren's time, as teacher-librarians, learning commons lead teachers, and other teachers need more in-depth mentoring through *coaching* in collaborative, planning, teaching, and assessing learning experiences. In two schools, Lauren *collaborates* with principals to work with the faculty in creating a shared vision for the approach and developing co-analysis of student learning data, including how to apply it to the WSSLC goals and actions and form steering teams. Occasionally Lauren's mentorship involves *consultation* with principals and presenting at staff meetings, or joining some of the steering team meetings to share or update information and resources on learning commons, for which Lauren *facilitates* professional learning time.

In one school, Lauren agrees to become a member of the steering team for the year, closely mentoring the appointed learning commons lead teacher. This teacher is highly skilled in technology for learning and enthusiastic about co-teaching with colleagues. Lauren coaches her in the approach through dialogue, discussion, and sharing planning tools and processes; she is also able to collaborate on a curricular project related to exploring forms of energy, mentoring both the lead teacher and classroom teachers involved directly, and connecting the school with a local wind farm as a partnership. Lauren is able to facilitate the learning commons lead teacher in learning about the "book side" of the commons, evaluating and selecting resources, and involving teachers and students in the process. Lauren coaches the school's library technician, who, although enthusiastic about the new approach and student education, expresses concern about her role or even her job status as change occurs. Through coaching Lauren is able to reassure the library technician that the learning commons is a team approach and needs and values all members. Through further coaching with both the library technician and the learning commons lead teacher, Lauren is able to help them work together as a team, with the library technician conducting a wide variety of technical and support operations in the physical and virtual learning commons, freeing the learning commons lead teacher and classroom teachers to focus on collaborative planning, teaching, and assessment.

Every six or eight weeks Lauren brings together the steering teams, turning her mentoring efforts toward the district community of practice. At meetings she provides updated information on resources such as free online reference resources and e-books from the state library, professional opportunities, and tools for areas she knows schools work on, such as co-teaching, designing physical and virtual learning spaces based on student needs, and gathering evidence of progress—especially student impact evidence. The meetings provide a forum for discussing timely issues or topics in small dialogue groups, and sharing co-taught learning projects, developments, successes, and challenges. If Lauren or another member recently attended a conference, the community of practice is a place to share what was learned. Guest speakers attend in person or through videoconference. Lauren designs a page on the district website for the community of practice, providing a virtual space that accommodates information, blogging, and sharing ideas, projects, and student work. The teams return to their schools as active on-site mentors.

As the year draws to a close, Lauren asks the schools to identify where they now fit on the continuum of themes and indicators from *Leading Learning: Standards of Practice for School Library Learning Commons in Canada* (Canadian Library Association, 2014b). She assesses her goals and actions of the year, and determines steps for next year.

Case Study 4 Discussion Questions

1. Discuss the pros and cons of Lauren's approach.
2. Will the district be able to continue the community of practice and implementation in schools if Lauren does not return for another year? Why or why not?
3. If Lauren returns for a second year, what do you think her next steps will be?
4. Would Lauren's approach work in your district? Why or why not? What additional suggestions do you have for district WSLLC mentoring?
5. Would Lauren's approach work in your school? What do you do differently or complementarily within your context?

Case Study 5:
Teacher-librarian mentoring teacher[*]

Cora is a new English teacher at an innovative school that serves students from grades 8–12. Mandated to follow the state curriculum and programs, the school strives to accomplish curricular success for all students enrolled by learning through the arts. Cora has not experienced this type of whole school pedagogical focus in her previous studies and practicum assignments to become an English teacher, but she uses the arts wherever possible during her practice and is very enthusiastic about her first teaching post. She is looking forward to teaching English through the arts to high school students, and she is curious about working with pre–high school students in the same setting as well.

Cora soon learns that teaching English to many classes of a variety of ages and learning needs each day involves a great deal of preparation and grading. With

---

[*]Based on a compilation of the author's experience.

nearly 200 students in seven classes, journals, papers, presentations, projects, and performances assigned in her first semester of teaching begin to overwhelm her. She worries about meeting the diverse needs of all of her students and staying afloat with class preparation and the many other duties expected of the faculty. When asked by her principal, department head, or colleagues, including the teacher-librarian, how it is going, Cora smiles and assures them everything is great.

The first professional learning day in the semester arrives, and Cora sees that it is going to be about something called the "Whole School Library Learning Commons" approach. She wonders what that means to her as a busy English teacher. She has been encouraging her students to use the school library to extend their reading choices beyond the ones she assigns. She has also noticed that the library has an exemplary collection of resources relating to the arts—visual art, music, drama, dance, literature resources in all formats—which would be great to explore once she finds more time. What more could the library offer, for the focus of a professional day?

At the professional day, the teacher-librarian shares information about the school library transforming into a learning commons, involving the whole school community. She states that the biggest indicator of the success of the transformation is the fact that most teachers on the faculty co-teach curricular experiences and events. She shares the article "Collaboration and Co-teaching—A New Measure of Impact" (Loertscher, 2014), which summarizes a study granted by the American Library Association, on the impact of co-teaching, planning, and assessment upon student learning. The study demonstrates how co-teaching makes a major impact on student learning. The principal remarks about how positive it is to hear this, and the vice principal adds that the effects of the learning commons approach are becoming evident in their own school through assessment data relating to outcomes that are co-planned, taught, and assessed in the learning commons approach, particularly in reading and writing assessments across the grades. The vice principal wonders: if their school replicates the study in the article to reflect on their successes and challenges with co-teaching, might their results be even better? Some of the teachers comment on how co-teaching impacts their practice and engages their students in deeper thinking and learning, and express thanks for the efforts of the teacher-librarian in working with them and mentoring them along the path of collaborative practice.

All of this is new to Cora, who has not previously encountered co-teaching or studies about it in her practicum or university studies. Some of the projects the faculty showcase on the professional day look wonderful—but, she wonders, how do they find time to do this along with teaching all their classes and fulfilling all of the other duties of a teacher? Cora feels more overwhelmed than ever.

As the professional day comes to a close, Cora sits glumly in her chair as the faculty disperse for the weekend. The teacher-librarian notices Cora remaining there, offers her a cup of tea, and sits down to talk with her. Cora shares that she has been feeling a little overwhelmed as a new teacher, and after hearing about co-teaching, she has no idea how, why, or when to engage in something like that. The teacher-librarian reassures her, acknowledging that the first few years of teaching can be overwhelming but that co-teaching is really something that helps. By working together, she and Cora can share the planning, teaching, and assessing, and learn from each other in supporting the students. She wonders whether Cora would be interested in joining her at a literature workshop the following week, relating to arts and English classes. Attending the workshop together has the potential to inspire ideas for Cora to approach co-teaching with the teacher-librarian for the first time—perhaps in an upcoming study of *Hamlet* that Cora is worried about planning and teaching, having heard the groans of many students when she announced it.

Cora and the teacher-librarian attend the workshop and follow up by arranging a few after-school planning sessions to begin the creation of a co-taught *Hamlet* project. Cora learns to use new teaching methods in the project, incorporating inquiry and research along with art and drama, as the teacher-librarian models and coaches alongside her. The students embrace the project, and the variety of assessments Cora and the teacher-librarian design with them prove how deep their learning is. As some students struggle, the teacher-librarian is there to provide additional support and guidance for them and suggestions for Cora in assisting them as well. The project concludes with an interactive *Hamlet* event—art, drama, music, writing—taking place in the physical learning commons and broadcast on the virtual commons for parents to attend or view online. Cora is delighted that even parents who might be uninterested in the activities of high schoolers appear to take an interest this time attending in person or online. Cora is also thrilled when the local public librarian, a colleague of the teacher-librarian, asks that some of the *Hamlet*-inspired sculptures her class had made be displayed at the public library for a few weeks. The principal remarks on how pleased he is with the *Hamlet* project, and also how glad he is to see Cora embracing co-teaching in the learning commons. Cora knows she has her new mentor, the teacher-librarian, to thank for that, and looks forward to co-planning the next project.

Case Study 5 Discussion Questions

1. Have you ever felt the way Cora did in her first teaching position? How did you deal with it?

2. Do you remember a great mentor for your teaching? What did you learn from him or her?

3. Does the approach of this teacher-librarian work in your school? Why or why not?

4. What additional suggestions would you have for the teacher-librarian, in mentoring Cora?

5. What do you do differently or complementarily within your context around teacher mentorship and the WSLLC?

Part II

ACCOUNTABILITY FOR LEARNING AND WSLLC

Chapter 4

AUTHENTIC ACCOUNTABILITY, STANDARDS, AND POLICIES

The fusion of learning, information, and technology presents dynamic challenges for teachers, school librarians, administrators, and students in 21st-century schools. Providing the best opportunities for children to learn and achieve in today's educational environment, and knowing that they've done well, is at the heart of quality teaching and learning, and is the driving force behind evidence-based practice. (Todd, 2008)

"Accountability" is not a word that educators generally find comfort with, as it brings to mind concerns or issues regarding the potential for over-emphasis on standardized testing and the "rating" of schools and educators. Yet the developmental concept of accountability for learning incorporates a balanced, strategic use of standardized test scores, along with a broad-based range of comparative student learning assessments. It is necessary for educators to utilize and understand these concepts when preparing targeted plans, goals, and strategic actions for student learning outcome achievement inclusive of all student needs. Accountability for learning informs the base for co-creating targets and measures, and for gathering empirical evidence to analyze whether the instructional designs and efforts in place for developing a learning commons approach most effectively impact student learning. How can educators know if their efforts and designs in implementing a learning commons approach make a difference to student learning, without employing accountability for learning principles and practices?

Accountability for learning (Reeves, 2004) is central to overall professional learning community work. Professional learning community work continues to be proven to be one of the most successful and sustainable school improvement initiatives of the past few decades (Eaker, Dufour, and Dufour, 2002). In a professional learning community, learning commons plans, goals, strategies, and actions infuse directly into school development or growth plans based on the needs of each student, as determined through continuous, collective student data analysis. The more collaborative the analysis of the data among educators is—along with collective setting of goals, targets, and measurements in a given school—the more impact it makes on instructional design to meet the multiplicity of student learning needs with curricular mandates throughout grades and across subject areas. In collective analysis of student data for instructional design, there is no separate "school library plan"; student data is incorporated into planning the learning commons approach.

Student learning data is best derived from at least three sources (this is known as triangulation of data), such as report card data, local and standardized test scores, recent assignments, and other broad-based assessment tools deemed important within the context of the school. Gathering and synthesizing student data information is less difficult today than in the past, as most of the information is available in digital format. Schools can acquire software programs to input data such as report card scores, and the software programs calculate the data so that educators can spend their time in overall pattern analysis, followed by collective instructional design planning. Together, educators pose and analyze questions such as the following:

- How did students fare on each type of assessment source being analyzed in the first semester? How did they do in the second semester?
- How do these site-based assessments compare with the previous year's standardized test results?
- What general and specific patterns and themes prevail?
- How does this information collectively focus refining and re-thinking aspects of current school library practices into implementing the learning commons approach?

Educators collectively analyzing student data naturally move into the realm of teacher or practitioner research, also known as action research. Engaging in action research skills and processes frames accountability for learning practices and processes. As a school principal, documented in Abilock, Harada, and Fontichiaro (2012, pp. 104–109), the faculty and I collectively learned to examine both qualitative and quantitative student data such as

- broad-based classroom assessment, including peer and student self-assessment;
- specific school library co-taught, planned, and assessed learning experiences;
- student, staff, and parent satisfaction surveys and focus groups;
- formal accountability satisfaction surveys from the ministry of education;
- quarterly and final report card grades; and
- standardized test results.

We participated in professional development activities related to working with and learning from standardized test data in relation to student learning patterns and particular gaps in determined curricular areas, examining both the school's own data and patterns as compared to district and provincial data. Where were students at the school experiencing challenge and success? What areas of curriculum and student performance did the school need to address more closely? How did this compare to similar areas in the district and province? Were there areas of curriculum being re-examined at the district or provincial level?

When analyzing the standardized test results at the school, the faculty identified and paid close attention to questions that had been recognized as having been taught through inquiry-based and collaboratively planned, taught, and assessed instruction, conducted as part of the developing school library program at the time. Teachers discovered that on these particular questions students had performed remarkably well. The teachers concluded that they needed to increase the co-planning, teaching, and assessing of school library learning experiences. It was also concluded that additional or re-thought professional learning and meeting time was needed so that time, a precious commodity in schools, was increasingly dedicated to accountability for learning practices and collaborative instructional design. Meetings and professional development activity structures focused on the continued collective analysis of student data, with ensuing time focused on collaborative instructional planning and design to move the school library into a developing learning commons approach. Teachers became increasingly comfortable with co-planning, teaching, and assessing school library learning experiences, yet mentioned the need for increased knowledge, mentoring, and coaching in order to become more comfortable and knowledgeable regarding practices and processes of accountability for learning—and its direct and continuous applications into practice.

It seemed ironic to have to re-think or create time to do what really is an educator's core work. What else took away time to collectively engage in student data analysis and instructional planning focused on current student context? We realized that we needed to examine what to give up or do less frequently or differently. As realizations such as these arose, creative solutions were forged. For instance, the deluge of information schools receive was shared through brief e-mails or notes to pertinent individuals as necessary, so that it did not take up meeting time. Meeting agenda items were assigned time limits; items running overtime were tabled to another forum, such as an after-school meeting if an issue involved everyone, or relegated to a particular professional learning community team or committee if only of direct interest there. Professional learning team meetings, including the school library professional learning team, replaced some of the general meetings. During informal discussions among educators, teachers consistently sought ideas and methods for improving or enhancing instruction, or discussed how best to support a student or group of students experiencing difficulties in learning. Soon this informal discussion moved into formal time, as it was realized that there wasn't another meeting agenda item more important than matching student needs with mandated curriculum, standards, and policies, and collectively improving in designing effective instruction.

Deep knowledge, exploration, and integration of curricular disciplines and mandated student learning outcomes by grade, matched with analysis of student profile, form the foundation for the emergence of the learning commons pedagogy and its accountability in impacting student learning. However, some educators feel uncertain or even resistant to exploring and implementing new approaches; they may wonder if the learning commons approach is yet "another new thing" they have no time for, as they have to "cover" curriculum. Some feel that the approach is just about the library—students signed out books there last week. Education specialists leading the learning commons approach, such as teacher-librarians, bring expertise in learning and teaching theory, including expertise in accountability for learning, broad-based assessment, curriculum, library information sciences, and technology for learning. Teacher-librarians often lead the introduction and implementation of the learning commons approach, through being accomplished in collaborative practice and leadership, countering resistance or uncertainty through mentoring, providing information and guidance, and advocating for and applying learning commons goals and actions within the accountability framework of the whole school plan. Ideally the teacher-librarian works with the principal and a steering team, using accountability for learning processes and incorporating techniques of action research—gathering evidence, analyzing data, sharing key resources through skillful professional development, co-creating the whole school vision and ownership, and refining and reflecting on development with colleagues, in a continuous cycle of leading and learning. Teacher-librarians "integrate research into practice every day. The whole process of teaching is research in action: using feedback and assessment data to evaluate the efficacy of a particular approach and adjusting practice accordingly" (Brooks Kirkland, 2015, October 13).

Evidence-based practice emphasizing student learning outcomes is not an unfamiliar concept in effective school librarianship practice (Todd, 2008), as schools continuously seek evidence that what they do in many areas, such as implementing the learning commons approach, best benefits students. "Evidence-Based Practice is not complicated. It is a simple process of paying attention to what you do and keeping a record of how that helps teachers and students. As Ross Todd explains, Evidence-Based Practice is 'knowing and showing how the school library program helps students learn'" (Ontario School Library Association, 2003). Todd's model for evidence-based practice is based on three dimensions:

- Evidence FOR practice—existing research
- Evidence IN practice—site-based actions
- Evidence OF practice—results

(Todd, 2009, p. 89)

Evidence FOR, IN, and OF practice adds dimension to the expectations of teacher-librarian practice and to the teacher-librarian's professional development needs in being able to share, lead, and apply evidence-based practice in school library to learning commons accountability.

Schools in every part of the world seek ways to demonstrate success and continually grow school library programs, increasingly moving into the learning commons approach. The International Federation of Library Associations and Institutions (IFLA) newly revised school library guidelines recommendation states that: "Evidence-based practice should guide the services and programs of a school library and provide the data needed for improvement of professional practice and for ensuring that the services and programs of a school library make a positive contribution to teaching and learning in the school" (Schultz-Jones and Oberg, 2015b, p. 11). Many curriculum standards and programs of study throughout the world evolve into holistic, inquiry-based frameworks—to "uncover" rather than "cover" curriculum—thus positioning the WSLLC approach, tied to accountability for learning, to benefit student achievement in breadth and depth of curriculum understanding, participatory learning, knowledge creation, and knowledge sharing.

STANDARDS AND POLICIES

As educators explore, implement, and engage in accountability for learning practices in the learning commons approach, they know about and align contextually designed instruction with related district, state, provincial, territorial, national, international, and professional standards and policies of the field. Standards and policies, based on best practice and research to date, provide direction and filters for best practice in contextual instructional design decisions at schools. It is important to align the learning commons pedagogy and planning with the overarching educational standards and curricular mandates expected, and then to ensure alignment with specific school library program and learning commons standards. Extensive resources available to support educators in using standards and policies are posted on most official district, government, educational, or institutional websites, and free or inexpensive for schools to access.

In the United States, the Common Core State Standards Initiative (National Governors Association Center for Best Practices and the Council of Chief State School Officers, 2016) in mathematics and English language arts/literacy (ELA) has been adopted by forty-three states, the District of Columbia, four territories, and the Department of Defense Education Activity (DoDEA). The Next Generation Science Standards (NGSS Lead States, 2015) has been adopted by thirteen states and the District of Columbia to date. Both documents provide measureable standards with extensive and practical implementation resources.

A brief prepared by the American Association of School Librarians, "Implementing the Common Core State Standards: The Role of the School Librarian" (2013) informs and supports all educators, not only the school librarian or steering team, with cross-curricular connections and continually updated resource supports for the Common Core State Standards at every level in the evolution of the school library program, applicable to the evolution of the learning commons approach. The brief lists ten initiatives that make the most difference to student learning, based on collaborative planning and teaching—central to the learning commons approach. The initiatives, listed below, include detailed checklists that describe each initiative, along with illustrative examples from a variety of schools.

> Ten initiatives that are thought to make the most difference in student learning based on collaborative planning and teaching:
>
> 1. Building reading, writing, speaking, and listening skills together across the curriculum.
> 2. Building appreciation of the best literature and informational materials together across the curriculum as a part of a literate culture.
> 3. Creating a school-wide participatory culture.
> 4. Building co-taught research projects in blended learning experiences.
> 5. Promoting interdisciplinary real-world problems, projects, and learning experiences that take advantage of rich information resources and useful technology tools.
> 6. Using technology to boost teaching and learning together.
> 7. Creating cultural experience across the school, community, and across the world.
> 8. Fostering creativity, innovation, play, building, and experimentation.
> 9. Assessing the results of collaborative learning experiences.
> 10. Managing the integration of classroom, school library learning commons, and technology tools.
>
>   (American Association of School Librarians, 2013, p. 12)

Preceding the Common Core implementation brief, national standards for school libraries in the United States, *Standards for the 21st-Century Learner* (American Association of School Librarians, 2007) were designed with an outcome-based vision for teaching and learning for school librarian leadership. The AASL standards are framed around four outcomes prevalent throughout best practice education and school library literature—standards or guidelines found in most state, province, territory, or national expectations:

1. Inquire, think critically, and gain knowledge.
2. Draw conclusions, make informed decisions, apply knowledge to new situations, and create new knowledge.
3. Share knowledge and participate ethically and productively as members of our democratic society.
4. Pursue personal and aesthetic growth.

            (American Association of School Librarians, 2007)

The AASL *Standards for the 21st-Century Learner* details a focus on "the learner, skills, dispositions in action, responsibilities, and self-assessment strategies," with benchmarks for putting the standards into action at each grade level with supporting resources (American Association of School Librarians, 2007). The AASL standards and the Common Core implementation brief provide educators with guidance and support on the journey to developing and implementing a learning commons approach. Additionally, the United States federal bill S.1177, "Every Student Succeeds Act," provides support by addressing literacy programs, including school libraries, with funding available for program and school librarian development—a move wholeheartedly endorsed by the American Library Association (Heltin, 2015).

A new national school library standards document was released in Canada through the Canadian Library Association (soon to be the Canadian Federation of Library Associations) in 2014. These standards remain unique at present, in that they directly focus on standards for a school library "learning commons." These learning commons standards premise a whole school community approach, so that any school can begin to apply the standards, whatever their circumstance or context. The standards publication, *Leading Learning: Standards of Practice for School Library Learning Commons in Canada* (Canadian Library Association, 2014b), merits study and use for setting direction and providing accountability when developing the learning commons approach. *Leading Learning* is a "transformational document" to use when exploring, moving toward, or further growing a school library to a school library learning commons approach. Use it for a variety of accountability for learning purposes, such as the following:

- an implementation guide for transition to a school library learning commons
- a measurement tool and framework for growth
- a framework for professional development
- a support for teacher-led action research

(Brooks Kirkland and Koechlin, 2015, pp. 45–47)

The development of *Leading Learning* began in 2003, when the Canadian Library Association supported and published national school library standards, *Achieving Information Literacy: Standards for School Library Programs in Canada* (Asselin et al., 2003, reprinted 2006). The new school library learning commons standards are not a revision of the previous standards—a seminal reference of their own with a dedicated vision, student information outcomes, and output standards—but a new digital format focused on the changing landscapes in education and the entire library community, with an outcome-based framework. The new standards align with general educational standards from best theoretical practice in twenty-first-century education, and provincial or territorial educational policies and standards. (Canada does not have national educational standards; each provincial or territorial education ministry sets out its own curricular mandates, standards, and policies.) These new and the previous standards, freely accessible, are posted on the website of the *School Libraries in Canada* online journal (Grose, 2016). With the exception of the cover image, *Leading Learning* is licensed under creative commons licensing for adaptation and use.

A key purpose in developing new school library learning commons standards in Canada was to provide an accountability framework—measures and standards—to those responsible for and committed to viable and successful school library development. In preparation, library leaders and practitioners across Canada contributed to a research retreat known as Treasure Mountain Canada (2016), an offshoot of Treasure Mountain United States (Loertscher, 2015c). The research retreat led to a preliminary vision for the standards, as well as formation of a national steering committee, focus group, and provincial and territorial committees organized through provincial and territorial school library associations (or representatives if there was not a school library association in the province or territory). The provincial and territorial volunteer committees that were formed to collaborate on the new standards project resembled as much as possible what an ideal school library learning commons steering team looks like: including teacher-librarians, principals, other school administrators or specialists, library technicians, classroom teachers, parents, students, and community librarians or other community representatives. A national steering committee and focus group, comprising members of the Canadian Library Association's School Library Advisory Committee and Voices for School Libraries Network, followed a roughly two-year timeline of collaborative writing and reviewing from proposal to completion. Resources and processes informing *Leading Learning* are available on a national project site that includes current news and resources relating to learning commons development (Voices for School Libraries Network, 2016).

Leading Learning provides dedicated insight into moving from a school library to a school library learning commons over a continuum of phases. The document defines the school library learning commons as

> a whole school approach to building a participatory learning community. The library learning commons is the physical and virtual collaborative learning hub of the school. It is designed to engineer and drive future-oriented learning and teaching throughout the entire school. Inquiry, project/problem-based learning experiences are designed as catalysts for intellectual engagement with information, ideas, thinking, and dialogue. Reading thrives, learning literacies and technology competencies evolve, and critical thinking, creativity, innovation and playing to learn are nourished. Everyone is a learner; everyone is a teacher working collaboratively toward excellence. (Canadian Library Association, 2014b, p. 5)

For accountability for learning purposes, the standards provide a continuum for learning commons development over four stages or phases: Emerging, Evolving, Established, and Leading into the Future (Canadian Library Association, 2014b, p. 8). Although an "exploring" stage is indicated in the document, it is not detailed; exploring schools use the Emerging phase to establish points of entry on the continuum. The document comprises five inter-connecting standards, denoted by different colors and symbols rather than numbers. This is intentional so that the standards are not seen or implemented as hierarchical, as schools will be at different points in each of the standard's themes and phases—for instance, Leading in some areas, Emerging in others. Contributors to the standards demonstrate a shared belief that the work of an effective school library learning commons is framed when the five core standards of practice weave together to generate dynamic learning. The standards of practice are best viewed in their entirety as a digital PDF (available on the Canadian Voices for School Libraries website). The summative statements for each standard are as follows:

- RED—Facilitating Collaborative Engagement to Cultivate and Empower a Community of Learners
- BLUE—Advancing the Learning Community to Achieve School Goals
- ORANGE—Cultivating Effective Instructional Design to Co-plan, Teach and Assess Learning
- GREEN—Fostering Literacies to Empower Life-Long Learners
- PURPLE—Designing Learning Environments to Support Participatory Learning

(Canadian Library Association 2014b, p. 8)

Most of the five standards have six "themes" of practice, with two having seven, and each theme has four indicators reflecting how the theme builds in practice across the phases of the continuum. For instance, in the Orange standard, "Cultivating Effective Instructional Design to Co-plan, Teach and Assess Learning," one of the themes is "Evidence-Based Practice," followed by four indicators of how evidence-based practice in growth looks when emerging, evolving, established, or leading into the future. Each indicator also provides "living links" to an example of the indicator in practice—one of the most practical and inspiring features of the new standards—labeled as "See it in Action." With five standards, six to seven themes each, and four indicators per theme, readers can access over 150 examples of "living links" from schools, school districts, and school library associations across the country and beyond. These examples provide a comprehensive resource for further understanding a particular indicator—or, if an indicator seems impossible to achieve, there is an example (or examples) to study, of educators implementing that very indicator "in action."

Leading Learning is influencing educational practice and policies throughout Canada, with interest developing in the United States and globally "with its unique approach, helping schools define success by impact on learning and providing an achievable framework for making that happen" (Brooks Kirkland, 2015, July 1). These school library learning commons standards bring essential questions forward, such as:

- How do goals currently become established at your school?
- How does instructional design happen?
- Do teachers plan, teach, and assess learning together?
- What kinds of learning environments do today's learners critically need?
- How is the community engaged in the approach, and do they understand the impact on student learning?

A detailed list of questions to facilitate dialogue about learning commons development and accountability appears in Appendix 1 of *Leading Learning*, titled "Standards Discussion Starters for Learning Leadership Teams" (Canadian Library Association, 2014b, p. 29).

In the United States, most states have a long history of developing and updating school library standards, such as those set by the California Department of Education (2010), the Texas State Library and Archives Commission (2005), or the South Dakota State Library (2010). The Massachusetts School Library Association (MSLA) lists *MSLA 2009 Massachusetts Recommended PreK–12 Information Literacy Standards* and "Rubrics for Evaluating School Library Programs" developed by MSLA in 2002 on its website "Standards and Rubrics" page (Massachusetts School Library Association, 2015). The Council of State School Library Consultants (2016) publishes a wiki listing, to date, approximately two-thirds of the states' information about curriculum or input standards for school libraries. Most of these standard sites have extensive resource links to support school libraries that facilitate a learning commons approach. Schools in the United States that don't see their state listed in this reference—or any school unsure about having state, provincial, territorial, or national school library standards or policies—can check with their government education or library departments for information.

The concept of state or provincial school library standards or policies incorporating "learning commons" is relatively new or rare at present. In Canada, Alberta is the first province or territory to have a "Learning Commons Policy," developed by the Ministry of Education in collaboration with provincial stakeholder committees and organizations, including the Alberta School Learning Commons Council (ASLC), over a period of six years. The ensuing approved learning commons policy was shared with schools in September of 2014. Schools in Alberta do not have a deadline to meet the policy, as it is recognized that school library to learning commons development takes different amounts of time for different schools, and is contextual and continual; and the important expectation from the policy is to begin. The Alberta Learning Commons Policy states,

> To support students in attaining the goals and standards as stated in the Ministerial Order on Student Learning, school authorities must ensure that students have access to a learning commons. A learning commons is an inclusive, flexible, learner-centered, physical and/or virtual space for collaboration, inquiry, imagination and play to expand and deepen learning. (Alberta Education, 2016)

The ASLC worked with and supported students in a media design class, along with their teacher, to create an informative video to view in relation to the policy. The video illustrates what a learning commons approach looks like across the grades (Alberta School Learning Commons Council, 2015).

Why is Alberta the only province or territory currently with a "Learning Commons Policy"? The province's education department website notes, "Research shows that students who have access to quality school library services, which a learning commons perspective enables, are more likely to exhibit advanced student achievement and literacy development" (Alberta Education, 2016). Alberta Education policies provide direction and mandates to schools; they do not provide the directions on "how to implement" but often do provide guidelines for implementation in line with the learning commons policy. Since there is no timeline for implementation of this policy, each school district in Alberta is planning implementation at its own pace. Schools begin implementing the learning commons policy by assessing where they currently practice, using measurement tools such as the policy guidelines or the themes and indicators from *Leading Learning*. The Alberta Education Learning Commons Policy guidelines and information could inform any school, district, state, province, or territory that may be considering or implementing the learning commons approach, or wanting to develop a policy relating to learning commons as over time they may develop school library standards and policies reflecting the learning commons approach. The policy and guidelines are on the Alberta Education website (Alberta Education, 2016).

ACCOUNTABILITY FOR CO-DESIGNING WSLLC GOALS AND ACTIONS

As discussed throughout this book, in order for the learning commons approach to be most effective in impacting student learning, educators in schools collaborate on developing goals and actions for infusion into the school development plan. They carefully examine and analyze student learning assessment data to set overall school goals and actions that dictate the goals and actions for the learning commons. Each educator contributes to developing goals and actions that support the learning commons in the school development plan.

The principal creates the conditions and accountability for learning processes, for teachers and teacher-librarians to set goals, actions, and strategies. Principals account for ensuring that teacher-librarians or learning commons lead teachers function as learning leaders and effective co-teachers, involving all students and all learning needs, and supports them in these functions by expecting teachers and other administrators or specialists to engage in and support co-teaching as well. The principal leads the faculty and enables time for analysis of student data to be examined, and the results of the data examination reviewed for co-planning of instructional design. Principals ensure that student assessment data is used to plan goals, actions, and strategies for greatest impact on student learning, and that the data is derived from at least three sources—standardized tests (if possible, identifying test questions relating to co-taught learning experiences), regular report card data, and pertinent anecdotal assessment samples. Principals examine and advise on decisions with the teacher-librarian and steering team, making certain that learning commons instructional decisions support the analyzed student needs from the school development plan and are reflected in co-planned and taught learning experiences. They highlight and discuss involvement and successes in the learning commons approach during teacher evaluation processes.

School administrators, such as the vice principal, department heads, guidance counselors, and others, support the principal in the above-mentioned development and implementation of the school plan that includes the WSLLC. Vice principals and guidance counselors often compile and conduct preliminary analysis of student assessment data in preparation for broader faculty analysis, goal setting, and action planning—in this case, focused on the learning commons approach. They ensure that the approach is successful and available to all students, and that it meets the diversity of student learning needs. Other school administrators ensure, through support and modeling, that teacher-librarians or lead learning commons teachers and classroom teachers impact student learning in the approach through co-planning, teaching, and assessing. Department heads bring expertise in their curricular areas and Common Core standards to co-planning and accountability.

In many schools the teacher-librarian is part of the administrative structure—and, with their expertise in the field, provide and employ tools for gathering evidence and accountability in developing the learning commons approach as an inclusive part of the school development plan. Teacher-librarians demonstrate that they act as leaders accountable to the learning community, for best practice in the approach. They communicate with the principal and other administrators often, sharing their vision, goals, and mission for a vibrant learning commons, and engaging support in involving the whole school in ownership and participation in its development. They work with the administrative team in bringing the approach to staff meetings, professional learning days, and events; surveying staff, students, and the community on an ongoing basis to further the growth of the learning commons approach; and creating and implementing a shared learning commons vision and goals that meet the context of the school and student profile. Teacher-librarians add the dimensions of evidence-based practice to their professional repertoire so that they lead and apply evidence FOR practice (the existing research), evidence IN practice (developing site-based research), and evidence OF practice (analyzing results) (Todd, 2009, p. 89), for equity in impacting student learning. A learning commons lead teacher prepares to approach learning commons accountability through engaging in professional development activities to gain expertise or certification in the field.

Classroom teachers bring expertise to accountability for learning regarding their students' needs through analysis of the broad-based assessment methods they have employed. Teachers join other classroom or subject teachers, the teacher-librarian or lead learning commons teacher, technology teachers, and administration, to collectively analyze similarities and differences among programs. They then relate this analysis to student needs, in preparation for setting collaborative school goals and outcomes, including the goals and outcomes for developing a learning commons approach. Teachers ensure that the learning commons physical and virtual pedagogical methods, spaces, and resources fit with and impact co-determined student needs. If teachers do not already co-plan, teach, and assess in a learning commons approach, they explore this process, which is proven to impact student success as a school grows in the learning commons pedagogical approach. Other specialist teachers—such as music or fine arts teachers, physical education teachers, and so on—teach many if not all of the students in some school settings and provide valuable insight into student need. In some settings, teacher specialists and school administrators have offices in or directly adjacent to the physical learning commons and engage in co-teaching, planning, and assessing with teacher-librarians and other teachers, to design rich and deep interdisciplinary learning experiences that the learning commons approach accounts for.

The approach itself is accountable, as it is introduced and developed for the purpose of impacting student learning at the center of school improvement. As the pioneers and authors of the learning commons concept say,

> continue to advocate for the Learning Commons concept to press deeply into the center of teaching and learning in a school. It needs to be at the heart of the learning community and be recognized for its contributions to education. The learning commons in the school evolves from a place of storage and retrieval of materials; it is now the transformation center where "all the good stuff" turns into learning. No longer should the teacher librarian and other specialists in the school find themselves on the outside of the classroom door knocking to get in; instead, by establishing a giant collaborative community, the virtual [and physical] learning commons elevates the classroom into participatory learning experiences within and beyond the school community. The Virtual [and physical] Learning Commons naturally knits the library resources, computer lab, reading skills center, technology center, and makerspace all into a truly new phenomenon that is bound to drive improved teaching and learning and thus school wide improvement. (Loertscher and Koechlin, 2012, p. 24)

Chapter 5

SELECTED ACCOUNTABILITY RESOURCES WITH STRATEGIES

Accountability, as a blueprint for professional integrity and significant outcome, is a commitment to growth through examining progress and practices. It brings alignment, innovation, collaboration, introspection, and effectiveness. Sustainable development through accountability requires a move from rhetoric to evidence, from a "tell me" framework to a "show me" framework, and from a process framework to an outcomes framework. (Todd, 2008)

In using or adapting the following selected resources and strategies when implementing the WSLLC approach—or others familiar to educators already in use in their schools—to develop practices and process of accountability for learning, continually remember to ask two crucial questions:

- How does the learning commons approach support each student's learning?
- How do we know it does?

WSLLC Accountability Resource 1:

Leading Learning: Standards of Practice for School Library Learning Commons in Canada (Canadian Library Association, 2014b) and *Standards for the 21st-Century Learner* (American Association of School Librarians, 2007)

WSLLC Accountability Strategy 1:

Introducing Standards through Symbols

The five inter-connecting school library learning commons standards from *Leading Learning: Standards of Practice for School Library Learning Commons in Canada* are assigned colors and symbols, rather than numbered, so as not to be seen or implemented as hierarchical. Schools implement at different places within each standard's themes—leading in some areas, emerging in others. The work of an effective learning commons approach is framed when the five core standards of practice weave together to generate dynamic learning. The standard symbols, carefully chosen over a long period of time, metaphorically represent the essence of the practice relating to the standard. One way to introduce or reflect upon these and other standards (such as AASL learner standards), and what they look like in development, is to introduce them by engaging steering teams, school faculties, students, and community using the following activity with individuals or in small groups.

Using the standards from *Leading Learning*, request that participants think about what each standard symbol suggests to them in relation to the learning commons approach. Then share the standards definition and have them reflect on how the definition compares to what they thought about the symbol. Have participants create a symbol reflecting their own learning commons practice for each CLA learning commons standard or AASL learner standard. Use the two charts on pages 61 and 62 to guide the activity.

Although the AASL standards do not directly use learning commons terminology, *Standards for the 21st-Century Learner* (American Association of School Librarians, 2007) is designed as an outcome-based vision for teaching and learning for school librarian leadership that aligns with the learning commons approach. Use the symbol activity to introduce or reflect upon the AASL standards, with the chart on page 62.

WSLLC Accountability Resource 2:

Leading Learning: Standards of Practice for School Library Learning Commons in Canada (Canadian Library Association, 2014b)

WSLLC Accountability Strategy 2:

Where Are We on the Learning Commons Journey?

The standards, themes, and indicators of *Leading Learning* are non-linear as schools move forward with the approach in different places at different times along the indicator growth continuum. Use the themes and indicator phases of these standards as a measurement tool to review where your school is on the school library to learning commons journey, and to set goals and actions for further development. Use the language from the standards to describe themes and phases of learning commons development for consistency when reviewing current plans and actions, in recording information about learning commons development in annual reports, and in advocacy materials as you collaborate to create shared understanding of the approach.

1.   Introducing Standards through *Leading Learning* Symbols

Leading Learning Standard	*Symbol	What does the symbol suggest to you, regarding the WSLLC?	Draw a symbol to represent the standard in your learning commons practice	Describe how to grow or further develop the standard concept in your school
RED Facilitating Collaborative Engagement to Cultivate and Empower a Community of Learners				
BLUE Advancing the Learning Community to Achieve School Goals				
ORANGE Cultivating Effective Instructional Design to Co-plan, Teach and Assess Learning				
GREEN Fostering Literacies to Empower Life-Long Learners				
PURPLE Designing Learning Environments to Support Participatory Learning				

Source: Canadian Library Association (CLA), 2014b, p. 8.

Have principals, teacher-librarians, and steering teams decide how to conduct a review of their school libraries to learning commons status, based on what they know has worked best in using accountability measures at their schools. One method is to have the principal survey the opinion of the entire faculty in reviewing school library to learning commons development, through accountability tools such as this or other standards documents, asking each faculty member to consider where they feel the school is on the continuum. When doing this type of surveying, request that participants also highlight themes, indicators, or concepts about which they desire more information or professional development. The general

2. Introducing AASL Standards through Symbols

Standards for the 21st -Century Learner Learners use skills, resources, and tools to:	Draw a symbol to metaphorically represent the standard.	Describe how this standard looks in your learning commons practice.	Describe how to grow or develop the standard further in your school.
1. Inquire, think critically, and gain knowledge.			
2. Draw conclusions, make informed decisions, apply knowledge to new situations, and create new knowledge.			
3. Share knowledge and participate ethically and productively as members of our democratic society.			
4. Pursue personal and aesthetic growth.			

Source: American Association of School Librarians, 2007.

survey provides the principal and steering team with information for planning next steps.

Another method is to form (if one has not already been formed) and engage the steering team initially in using the standards continuum charts to map out where they believe the school is on the school library to learning commons continuum, prior to bringing the activity to the broader faculty for discussion and verification of the question "Where is our school now with the learning commons approach, and where do we want to go?" Use the following steps with *Leading Learning* as an overall surveying tool.

- View the learning commons standards charts online, and print copies for participant response (Canadian Library Association, 2014b, pp. 11–20). The online version allows participants to view the "See it in Action" links to further clarify or illustrate a learning commons indicator.
- Share the standard definition, as well as its first theme and indicators. For example, the "red" standard, "Facilitating collaborative engagement to cultivate and empower a community of learners," is defined thus:

The library learning commons plays a key role in cultivating and facilitating collaboration to provide rich experiential learning opportunities. It provides not only a physical space to develop skills and engage learners, but is also a portal to virtual connections, both local and global. It is important to acknowledge the diverse needs and contributions of all players within the school learning commons community, both in terms of resource formats and access to information and collaboration opportunities. Local, regional and global connections and collaborations are a vital part of progressive, future-oriented learning environments (Canadian Library Association, 2014b, p. 11).

- Its first theme is "Vision for Learning," with the following indicators:
  ○ Emerging: Library Learning Commons (LLC) is explored by the school to address shifts in learning needs and environments.
  ○ Evolving: LLC is evolving as a whole school approach to collaborative learning.
  ○ Established: LLC drives school wide collaborative teaching and learning.
  ○ Leading into the Future: LLC builds learning communities and is responsive to evolving school, district and global changes.
  (Canadian Library Association, 2014b, p. 11.)
- Ask each participant to use a check mark on the chart to indicate where they believe the school currently is on the "Vision for Learning" continuum—Exploring? Emerging? Evolving? Established? Leading into the Future? If unsure, view "See it in Action" clips to provide further clarification of the indicator.
- Go on to the next theme.

Explore one standard at a time, since there are five standards with six or seven themes and four indicators per theme—or spend part of a professional day going through all of the standards. Some faculties or steering teams may go through the charts fairly quickly, depending on their context with school libraries and learning commons. Collate responses to determine where most faculty members believe the school is in the continuum of learning commons development phases, and also where more information or professional development is indicated. Share the results and discuss next steps and plans for moving along a learning commons continuum.

WSLLC Accountability Resource 3:

"Learning Standards and Common Core State Standards Crosswalk" (American Association of School Librarians, 2016c)

WSLLC Accountability Strategy 3:

The Big Picture

Collectively discuss the alignment of school library to learning commons plans with school development plans and district or state standards and policies, by focusing on one or more core curricular outcomes from a chosen discipline. Connect the selected curricular outcomes with education and school library/learning commons standards. A key resource to use with this strategy is the American Association of School Librarians (AASL) "Learning Standards and Common Core State Standards Crosswalk" (American Association of School Librarians, 2016c). The crosswalk tables are designed to align AASL *Standards for the 21st–Century Learner* (American Association of School Librarians, 2007) with the Common Core Standards (National Governors Association Center for Best Practices and Council of Chief State School Officers, 2010). The crosswalk tables offer valuable connections for teacher-librarians and all educators implementing the learning commons approach, to use in collaborative instructional design.

Use Table 5.1, "Aligning WSLLC Strategies with Education and School Library/Learning Commons Standards," to align student data analysis, school development goals and outcomes, and selected standards of practice.

WSLLC Accountability Resource 4:

A Guide to Support Implementation: Essential Conditions (Alberta's Education Partners, 2010, Rev. July 2012)

WSLLC Accountability Strategy 4:

Reflection, Evidence, Planning

The school development plan or growth plan is where student data is examined and learning goals set. Embed the learning commons approach implementation and sustainability plans within these planning structures, and review and reflect upon them in an inclusive, annual, and continual process. An online guide, A Guide to Support Implementation: Essential Conditions (Alberta's Education Partners, 2010, Rev. July 2012), is available for schools to use in facilitating this process. The guide is based on seven conditions deemed essential for implementing new curriculum or educational initiatives. These seven conditions were determined by a working group of educational organizations derived from "research, literature and promising practices." Conditions that the group deemed essential for successfully implementing curriculum or other educational initiatives found in the guide are "shared vision, leadership, research and evidence, resources, teacher professional growth, time and community engagement." Use the charts in the online guide to record gathered evidence of implementation of the learning commons approach and to set goals and actions based on the evidence. Add descriptors unique to the context of your school.

Use the Essential Conditions descriptors to determine whether the learning commons development in your school meets conditions deemed essential for implementation and sustainability success. Have the principal lead the use of the Essential Conditions self-assessment tool as a broad survey instrument early in the year, requesting that each staff member reflect upon the questions and

Table 5.1　Aligning WSLLC Strategies with Education and School Library/Learning Commons Standards

NATIONAL K–12 EDUCATIONAL STANDARDS	STATE/ PROVINCE/ TERRITORY OR SCHOOL DISTRICT STANDARDS	SCHOOL LIBRARY LEARNING COMMONS STANDARDS OF PRACTICE	WSLLC SCHOOL PLAN STRATEGIES
		(e.g., CLA, 2014*) *Facilitating Collaborative Engagement to Cultivate and Empower a Community of Learners.*	
		Designing Learning Environments to Support Participatory Learning	
		Advancing the Learning Community to Achieve School Goals	
		Fostering Literacies to Empower Lifelong Learners	
		Cultivating Effective Instructional Design to Co-plan, Teach, and Assess Learning	

*Leading Learning: Standards of Practice for School Library Learning Commons in Canada (Canadian Library Association, 2014b).

respond to them, sharing the evidence that led to their response and adding ideas to contribute for going forward. The principal works with the steering team (or forms one if not in place) to examine the responses and determine next steps. Or have the teacher-librarians, learning commons lead teacher, or steering team use the Essential Conditions self-assessment tool to reflect on learning commons development, share their reflections with the principal, and decide together how to use the essential conditions with the faculty to gather information, dialogue, input, and plans, to build shared ownership of the approach. Use descriptor questions related to learning commons development and essential conditions for implementation such as those adapted to the learning commons approach, listed below, when self-assessing or surveying. Add other descriptors as needed to suit your context.

Shared Vision

- Does the school have a shared vision for the WSLLC? If so, what is it? If not, how do we develop it?
- Is the learning commons approach integrated into the student learning goals and outcomes of the school plan? How? If not, how does the approach support our student learning goals and outcomes?
- Do educators in the school collaborate to build learning commons pedagogy into existing resources and learning programs? If yes, provide an example. If not, how do we accomplish this or continue to grow with it?

Leadership

- Does the principal lead the faculty in adopting and implementing the approach in collaboration with a teacher-librarian or learning commons lead teacher?
- Is there a WSLLC steering team? If so, is the team representative of the school community? If not, how do we form a steering team?
- Is there a learning commons action plan designed with the help of the steering team?

Research and Evidence

- Does the approach support all students in the school through continual analysis of student assessment data?
- Is learning commons literature shared, updated, discussed, and considered in decision-making?
- Is learning commons development archived using collaborative technologies such as surveys, spreadsheets, or Google docs?

Resources

- Is a resource collection plan outlined, with an outcomes-based budget focused on co-determined student learning needs?
- Are learning resources accessible to students and staff 24/7? If not, what is needed to make this happen?
- Do the learning commons physical and virtual spaces reflect collectively designed learning environments based on student learning needs?

Teacher Professional Growth

- How is learning commons professional learning provided? How do we provide or enhance it?
- How do we document and measure professional growth goals and outcomes for the approach?
- What does success in the approach mean for teacher professional growth?
- What does success in the approach mean for students?
- What is someone able to observe as part or all of the WSLLC goals are reached?

Time

- Do flexible timetables and scheduling facilitate co-planning, teaching, and assessing?
- Do students have extensive time for inquiry-based learning, participatory learning, collaborative knowledge building?

Community Engagement

- How is the approach and its impact on student learning understood throughout the learning community?
- How is success with the approach celebrated and communicated throughout the learning community?

WSLLC Accountability Resource 5:

The Teacher Librarian's Toolkit for Evidence-Based Practice (Ontario School Library Association, 2003)

WSLLC Accountability Strategy 5:

Design and Document Instructional Strategies

The Teacher Librarian's Toolkit for Evidence-Based Practice provides educators with an expanded repertoire of ideas, tools, and strategies dedicated to gathering and sharing evidence of student success, focused on best-practice school library learning experiences, which a learning commons approach facilitates. By examining, discussing, and analyzing student learning information together, educators can make the most effective decisions for instructional design. How does the learning commons approach best support what students need now and going into the future? What evidence do we examine? What does evidence such as report cards, tests, and broad-based assessment results tell us about each student's learning? Which learning commons indicators do we establish or extend further to support these learning needs?

Use Table 5.2 as a tool to record student learning evidence examined through an identified curricular outcome. Record gaps identified from analyzing the evidence, and set goals or targets with learning commons strategies identified to reach them. For example, a common focus for schools is improving student learning outcomes

Table 5.2   WSLLC Assessment for Learning Accountability Planner

Student Learning Outcome:

Evidence/Measures:

Identified Gap from Evidence Analysis:

Goal or Target:

Bring _____ scores up _____% by _____

WSLLC Strategies to Achieve Goal or Target:

related to reading development. Evidence to examine includes standardized reading test scores, report card data, various other reading tests and measures, and even the number of collaboratively planned, taught, and assessed literacy projects. If a school discovers reading scores to be 20% lower than standardized test norms, they set targets to see that percentage rise, perhaps by 20% within two years, by initiating a number of reading growth strategies such as increasing collaborative literacy projects.

WSLLC Accountability Resource 6:

Professional Growth Plans (tutorials; Alberta Teacher's Association, 2016)

WSLLC Accountability Strategy 6:

WSLLC Professional Learning Goals

Professional growth goals relating to teaching standards and certification are required in most if not all school districts, to be implemented and reviewed on an ongoing basis. Resources to support setting and achieving professional goals include professional learning tools and events provided by national, state, provincial, or territorial professional organizations. The United States National Education Association (NEA), with affiliates in each state, has a new policy statement on teacher evaluation and accountability that "sets forth criteria for the types of teacher evaluation and accountability systems necessary to ensure a high quality public education for every student" (NEA, 2015a). NEA provides an online section of "tools and ideas" (NEA, 2015b) for teacher professional learning, including a wide variety of teaching strategies. Each state also has requirements for preparation and procuring of teacher-librarian certification (American Association of School Librarians, 2016d).

In Alberta the teacher association provides online tutorials based on literature and research from the teacher professional growth field, to guide teachers in their professional growth plan processes following four key steps. First, educators review their teacher or teacher-librarian policy and certification regulations. Second, educators spend time reflecting on their current professional practice. Third, they develop a professional growth plan. Fourth and finally, educators prepare for a successful implementation and review of the plan (Alberta Teacher's Association, 2016). Tutorials on the site include sample professional growth plans, templates, and charts to guide educators in setting "SMART" goals:

S—specific, significant, stretching

M—measurable, meaningful, motivational

A—agreed upon, attainable, achievable, acceptable, action-oriented

R—realistic, relevant, reasonable, rewarding, results-oriented

T—time-based, timely, tangible

(Alberta Teacher's Association, 2016)

Set a "SMART" professional goal focused on the learning commons approach. Start by asking the following questions:

- What is accomplished by achieving this goal?
- What do I find energizing and look forward to focusing on by setting this goal?

When reflecting on the goal, consider:

- What have I accomplished with this goal?
- What do I look forward to focusing on going forward?

Create an in-person forum to comfortably share with colleagues and discuss setting and reflecting upon the WSLLC goals. Do this in teams or grade groups as part of a meeting or professional day, or online on a dedicated school or district intranet page, or by meeting with a formal or informal mentor.

WSLLC Accountability Resource 7:

"Assessing Effective School Library Learning Commons Indicators: What Do They Look Like? What Questions Can Help Us Assess Where We Are?" (Brown and Sykes, 2016)

WSLLC Accountability Strategy 7:

"Look-Fors," Strategies, Assessment Questions

The paper in this strategy, prepared for TMC 4 (Treasure Mountain Canada, 2016), addresses the components of a school library as transitioning into an effective learning commons approach using selected themes from *Leading Learning: Standards of Practice for School Library Learning Commons in Canada* (Canadian Library Association, 2014b). Encourage principals and other administrators, teacher-librarians, steering teams, and faculties to use and examine in detail observations and questions to address when implementing or assessing a learning commons approach. Although there are 32 themes in *Leading Learning*, the 14 selected themes in the paper reflect components most educators associated with school libraries are familiar with, including the following:

- The learning commons leadership team
- Collaborative planning, teaching, and assessment
- Instructional partnerships
- Inter-agency collaboration
- Information literacy
- Engaging through inquiry
- Literacy and literary and cultural appreciation

- Designing for responsive print and digital collections
- Technology for learning
- Technology competencies

Descriptions for assessing the themes, in the form of questions or lists, depict what the component looks like (observables), strategies for implementing the component, and guiding questions for assessing components.

Use the paper in a workshop or meeting by selecting themes over time to focus on. Have facilitators (principal, teacher-librarian, steering team members) conduct a quick survey of which themes most interest the faculty in order of priority, or prioritize based on where you are with learning commons development. Once a theme is ready to be explored, choose a time at a staff meeting or professional learning event and request that the faculty brainstorm to complete the sentence stems using a print or digital version of the chart below. The chart will help faculty examine what they "look for" in addressing the concept; what strategies they currently use to implement it, or what they would suggest the school use to address it; and what assessment questions apply to the school. Following the brainstorm and discussion, share the actual lists from the paper "Assessing Effective School Library Learning Commons Indicators" (Brown and Sykes, 2016) and other sources as applicable, to compare with the brainstormed lists. Highlight additions from the chart, and use them as ideas for guiding future learning commons design collaboration. Choose other themes from *Leading Learning* that were not selected for the article, or themes from other sources, to create additional "look-fors, strategies, and assessment questions."

Assessing Effective School Library Learning Commons Indicators Chart

Selected WSLLC Theme: _____	School List	Additions from lists in: "Assessing Effective School Library Learning Commons Indicators" (Brown and Sykes, 2016)
What does _____ look like?	Our observables:	
Suggested Strategies for _____ Implementation	Our implementation strategies:	
How is _____ assessed?	Our methods of assessing:	

WSLLC Accountability Resource 8:

"School Librarianship and Evidence-Based Practice: Perspectives, Progress and Problems" (Todd, 2009)

WSLLC Accountability Strategy 8:

Evidence Collectors

In the article "School Librarianship and Evidence-Based Practice: Perspectives, Progress and Problems," the author references three dimensions of evidence-based practice: evidence FOR practice (existing research), evidence IN practice (site-based actions), and evidence OF practice (results; Todd, 2009, p. 89). Read the article together as a steering team or faculty, and follow up by exploring the following questions over a series of professional learning meetings:

- What evidence (published research) do we know about that relates the learning commons approach to enhancing educational practice? What does the published research tell us? (Note: In chapter 6 of this book, school library and learning commons published research and recommended summaries of this research are discussed. For the purpose of this activity, use the poster and/or video from "School Libraries Impact Studies" [Library Research Service, 2013] and/or read the article "School Library Research Summarized: A Graduate Class Project. Rev. Ed." [Kachel and Graduate Students of LSC 5530 Mansfield University, 2013].)

- What evidence do we gather in our own school, in transforming practice through the school library to a learning commons approach? How do we do this?

- What do we learn from our own school evidence about our learning commons approach and student achievement results? How does our evidence compare to the research we examine?

- What next steps do we take based on what we have learned by comparing our learning commons development evidence with the published research?

WSLLC Accountability Resource 9:

Leading Learning: Standards of Practice for School Library Learning Commons in Canada (Canadian Library Association, 2014b, p. 16)

WSLLC Accountability Strategy 9:

Where Do We See Ourselves in Evidence-Based Practice?

The evidence-based practice theme is part of the school library learning commons standard "Cultivating Effective Instructional Design to Co-Plan, Teach and Assess Learning" (Canadian Library Association, 2014b, p. 16). Use the following chart to discuss and determine where your school is on this school library learning commons evidence-based practice continuum. Share the "See It in Action" examples and address your own school goals in moving forward through these phases of development.

Where do we see ourselves in WSLLC evidence-based practice?

Where is our school on the continuum of evidence-based practice phases* in developing the WSLLC?	What examples from our school support your response?	Goals and actions for moving forward through the phases
EMERGING: *Teacher-librarians/LLC teachers work with the LLC leadership team to review the LLC learning experiences and set goals for improvement.*		
EVOLVING: *Teacher-librarians and teachers build and share their professional knowledge of approaches and environments to support inquiry learning and assess its effectiveness.*		
ESTABLISHED: *Teacher-librarians initiate collaborative action research with teachers to build best practice strategies and approaches to learning in the LLC and assess its effectiveness.*		
LEADING INTO THE FUTURE: *Teacher-librarians contribute their knowledge of best practice results in their LLC to the broader education community.*		

*Canadian Library Association (CLA), 2014b, p. 16.

Part III

READING AND RESEARCH ON WSLLC

Chapter 6

SCHOOL LIBRARY TO LEARNING COMMONS LITERATURE AND RESEARCH

Today, many school libraries are being designed as "learning commons" in response to users' involvement in "participatory culture," which extends the users' roles from consumers of information to creators of information. (Schultz-Jones and Oberg, 2015, p. 32)

The background to the emergence of school library to learning commons literature and research resides in an extensive literature and research base of more than fifty years, focused on school libraries and teacher-librarianship. As pointed out previously, however, this type of literature and research is not well known to many educators outside these fields. "Learning commons" literature and research is relatively new, and schools exploring the approach will often begin with familiarity or background knowledge relating to school library literature and research. This chapter highlights several key school library literature and research sources for background information, yet places greater emphasis on the developing resources focused on the learning commons approach.

School library literature and research describe best practice in school librarianship as also involving a whole school approach, a constructivist base, and a focus on collaborative planning, teaching, and assessment. Ensuing research on the impact of school libraries on student learning shows higher achievement test scores on both formative and summative assessment studies, no matter the socio-economic or community education level. These best-practice school libraries demonstrate active learning programs that contribute to making the school library a vital center of inquiry and collaboration in schools, and the results dependent upon best teacher-librarianship practice, in which a teacher-librarian actively collaborates in all aspects of instruction with each of the classes and teachers in the school.

Despite the extensive research on the impact on student achievement of school library programs led by dynamic teacher-librarians, when examining literature related to school libraries, it will be pointed out that many school districts eliminate professional teacher-librarians for a number of reasons. One reason is declining budgets, also seen in reductions in arts and athletic programs. Another reason is the belief that web technology replaces a "tired concept" (Loertscher, 2014, p. 8)— namely, school libraries and teacher-librarians. However, most schools in Canada and the United States, including new schools, have and continue to build a dedicated physical space for a school library (also referred to as a school library media center) and, increasingly, space for a "learning commons." These dedicated spaces cost plenty to resource and maintain, operating with decreasing staffing of both certificated and technical or clerical personnel. The school library in some cases functions as a space with things in it such as books and other resources; rather than as an active, collaborative learning approach that brings the space to life within and beyond its walls throughout the school. As discussed in previous chapters, this active approach is interwoven within the overall school development plans, based on analysis of student learning needs aligned with curricular outcomes and mandates. Once student needs are collectively established, educators plan, teach, and assess collaboratively, ideally with a teacher-librarian, to impact the learning needs of their students. Planning is not *in addition to* a school plan; it is an immersive blending of effective school and school library practice—student-centered, collaborative, and innovative; implemented through collective instructional design in rich physical and virtual learning environments. This rich environment, whether in real or archived time, physical or virtual, is "relentlessly focused on learning" (Oberg, 2014b) and not on artificial collections or unhelpful rules, with the physical and virtual spaces operating simultaneously to support each student's learning, as determined through accountability for learning practices. Educators developing these rich learning environments continually revisit the question: How can the learning commons approach support our student learning goals and outcomes?

Metaphors for effective school library programs in the literature include the "heart or hub" of the school, a learning laboratory, a studio, or even the "great room" of the school, again often due to the talent and skill of an effective teacher-librarian along with the supporting technical and clerical personnel. Transitioning to a learning commons approach extends the metaphor to imagining the learning commons as perhaps a "fifth wall" in the classrooms, seamlessly breaking down isolation in instructional practice throughout the school. Another metaphor for school library to learning commons—and, by extension, classrooms—is the "kitchen," the sense of a place to create or "make":

> We need to stop thinking of the library as a store—a place to "get stuff"—and start thinking of it as a kitchen—a place to "make stuff." Libraries are becoming maker-spaces, giving all students access to workstations with fast processing speed,

adequate memory, and software for video and photo editing, music production, voice recordings, computer programming, multimedia composition, and even 3-D printers. (Rixon, 2014)

Best practices in instructional design for learning and teaching create within this maker milieu a focal point for student engagement with information, ideas, critical and creative thinking, making meaning, and dialogue across the disciplines of curriculum.

Engaging with information, ideas, critical and creative thinking, making meaning, and dialogue across the disciplines of curriculum requires quality resources in different formats. Resources for the learning commons are designed as "responsive print and digital collections" (Canadian Library Association, 2014b, p. 20) and cultivated to support identified student needs from the school plan. Whether print or digital, school library and learning commons literature notes that educators evaluate and select quality fiction and non-fiction resources in many formats for students of all ages and abilities—including print books—to meet learning needs and interests. It sometimes appears that books in print form disappear as school libraries transform into learning commons. Different cognitive processes are required for reading in print and digital forms, and both are necessary. As collection development based on student need and curricular change occurs, outdated or unsuitable resources in the learning commons are removed, based on authoritative resource evaluation criteria. In some cases it can seem as though many books are gone if the collection is newly assessed and being updated, as educators consider the quality, purpose, and best format for new resource purchases.

As educators engage in exploring and implementing a learning commons approach, familiarity with newly developing literature and research focused on learning commons provides information and guidance for discussion, reflection, and collectively moving forward with action plans. Historically, the term "commons" derives from the medieval gathering space or market: "The village green, or 'common,' was traditionally a place to graze livestock, stage a festival, or meet neighbors. This concept of social utility underlies the philosophy of the modern learning commons, which is a flexible environment built to accommodate multiple learning activities. Designing—or redesigning—a commons starts with an analysis of student needs and the kind of work they will be doing" (Lippincott and Greenwell, 2011). Academic libraries were one of the first modern institutions to start transforming libraries into user-faced information commons using the term "learning commons." Public libraries followed, developing community-centered learning commons approaches. School, public, and academic libraries share common goals and aspirations such as literacy and lifelong learning, and also serve unique purposes and mandates. School libraries support kindergarten to grade twelve programs of study; post-graduate libraries support research and study for their programs and students; and public libraries support the broad public focus, providing free access to collections, resources, and services to patrons of all ages, to obtain information relating to personal, educational, and professional needs. In Alberta, Canada, the combined library community worked together to develop a

Collaborative Library Policy that "respects the diverse roles and services that local public, school, and post-secondary libraries occupy in Alberta's diverse communities; while enabling stakeholders and government to work towards more efficient and effective library service delivery" (Alberta Municipal Affairs, 2013).

The American Association of School Librarians (AASL) and state or provincial school library associations provide access to a great and growing amount of information, literature, and research regarding resources, school libraries, teacher-librarianship, and increasingly, learning commons. The American Association of School Librarians (AASL) website is where to access the *Standards for the 21st-Century Learner* (discussed in chapter 4) as well as extensive research, or links to research, regarding the effectiveness of quality school library programs and student achievement. A comprehensive bibliography is developed to support *Leading Learning: Standards of Practice for School Library Learning Commons in Canada* (Canadian Library Association, 2014b), containing many key references related to school libraries and school library to learning commons, and links to the action examples from schools and teacher-librarians. School library associations within states or provinces and territories in most countries retain important directional documents and resources and links to national information. International information and literature about school libraries or learning commons can be accessed through the International Association of School Librarianship (IASL; 2016).

When examining the literature of school libraries and school library to learning commons, access the major research studies related to impacting student achievement. Knowing about these major studies, and sharing summaries of the results with the faculty and greater community, demonstrates the need to move forward and embrace a learning commons pedagogical approach that provides students with a distinct advantage for success. School library impact studies have been conducted and documented over at least twenty years in twenty-one American states, Ontario, and British Columbia (Library Research Service, 2013) and repeated in their original state of Colorado (Lance, 2015). These studies support a similar direct correlation between advanced student achievement and quality school libraries with teacher-librarian leadership, which a learning commons approach supports. The Library Research Service provides both summary and detailed information on school library student impact studies, including an infographic poster demonstrating the links to improved standardized reading test scores, a seven-part video series discussing the impact of school libraries on student achievement, "fast fact" reports from the various studies, and the full study reports.

Most educators appreciate summaries of research studies, especially when first being introduced to them or when being introduced to an unfamiliar field. A succinct summary of the school library impact studies research is compiled in "Research Foundation Paper: School Libraries Work!" (3rd ed.), which summarizes these research results to 2008, noting, "A substantial body of research since 1990 shows a positive relationship between school libraries and student achievement. The research studies show that school libraries can have a positive impact on student achievement—whether such achievement is measured in terms of reading scores, literacy, or learning more generally. A school library program that is adequately staffed, resourced, and funded can lead to higher student achievement regardless of the socio-economic or educational levels of the community" (Scholastic Library Publishing, 2008, p. 10).

Another summary of school library impact studies is published by students in the School Library and Information Technologies Graduate Program, Mansfield University, Mansfield, PA, as part of their course work since 2011. Included in the 2013 publication compiled by the instructor (Kachel, 2013) is a chart depicting "school library program components and the states/province in which they were found to have a positive association with student achievement," as well as concise summaries of the major findings of the past ten years in the areas of "school library staffing, collaboration, instruction, scheduling, access, technology, collections, budget, professional development, and achievement gap." Kachel affirms,

> Clearly, the studies confirm that quality school library programs with full-time, certified librarians and library support staff are indicative of and critical to student achievement. In fact, quality school library programs may play an even greater role in providing academic support to those students who come from economically disadvantaged backgrounds. In closing the achievement gap and assuring that all students are prepared with the 21st century skills they need to succeed, school leaders and librarians need to embrace this body of research and foster school library programs that can make a difference in student learning. Schools that support their library programs give their students a better chance to succeed. (Kachel, 2013, p. 5)

Although major research studies, international research studies, and literature on school libraries are extensive, as noted, many educators outside of the school library field do not know about them, nor realize the potential of the school library learning commons approach in impacting school reform and student success advantage. A contributing factor is that such research and its results find publication and sharing in school library journals and other school library media forums, and rarely in teacher, administrator, or even technology journals and forums, other educational association forums, or education university degree programs. In order to advance the learning commons approach development and build shared vision and understanding of its impact on student learning success, it is enlightening and beneficial to collectively share the major research summaries, and follow any new developments. Library Research Services founder, director, and key researcher Keith Curry Lance poses three critical questions for educators to consider when conducting educational research: "How can we ensure that students leave school having learned how to learn? Having learned how to know when they need information? Where to find it and how to know if it's any good or not?" (Achterman, 2007).

Literature directly focused on school library learning commons has come into view principally within the last decade, with the publication of the first and second editions of *The New Learning Commons: Where Learners Win! Reinventing School Libraries and Computer Labs* (Loertscher, Koechlin, and Zwaan, 2008, 2011b). Emerging from literature, research, and best practice in school libraries and teacher-librarianship, the fundamental vision, as well as burgeoning literature and research reflecting the learning commons approach, arose and continues to build notably through the progressive leadership, inspiration, and publications of Dr. David Loertscher. Loertscher is a professor at the School of Library and Information Science at San Jose State University, former co-editor of *Teacher Librarian* journal, and former president of the American Association of School Librarians (AASL), among his many other accomplishments. Loertscher often collaborates with outstanding educator Carol Koechlin, an independent educational consultant from Toronto, Canada, who was the writing coordinator and contributing author for *Leading Learning: Standards of Practice for School Library Learning Commons in Canada* (Canadian Library Association, 2014b). These learning commons pioneers and leaders first define learning commons as

> a learning "space" that is both physical and virtual. As you might guess, a Learning Commons is about common physical and virtual places to experiment, practice, celebrate, learn, work, and play. But a Learning Commons is more than a room. Much more than that, it calls for the creation of new environments that improve learning. It is about changing school culture and about transforming the way learning and teaching occurs. (Koechlin, Rosenfeld, and Loertscher, 2010, p. 9)

Publications by Loertscher and Koechlin—together and with various collaborators, listed in this book's bibliography—provide learning commons pedagogical background and implementation resources, ideas, and practical tools for schools to forge forward in the learning commons approach. Loertscher and Koechlin design and continually update a companion virtual learning commons website to support the learning commons books (Loertscher and Koechlin, 2016a), with new and emerging resources, literature, research, innovation, exemplars, and news.

Loertscher and Koechlin are primary experts and "names to know" in the school library to learning commons approach, for educators to familiarize themselves with as they embark on learning commons journeys. Loertscher and Koechlin ground school library to learning commons pedagogy in knowledge building and collaboration:

> Knowledge building is a central focus of the learning commons program. The program of the learning commons is to use the power of information and technology, the physical space of the learning commons as an extension of the classroom, and the curriculum of the various classrooms, to push excellence in the school through effective collaboration. The emergence of collaborative technologies, the opening of quality information and multimedia resources, and quality instructional designs, allow classroom teachers new opportunities to develop super learning experiences jointly with the specialists of the school. Teacher librarians, teacher technologists, reading specialists, teachers of the gifted, and special education teachers stand ready to combine forces to demonstrate that co-teaching and integrated instruction are far superior to isolated one-person teaching strategies. Knowledge building can happen as a face-to-face experience, a totally online experience, or a combination of both. (Loertscher and Koechlin, 2016a)

According to Loertscher, Koechlin, and fellow contributor Zwaan, the learning commons approach accommodates two major functions. First,

Open Commons—the place, both physical and virtual where classes, individuals, small groups, events are scheduled to benefit from the support and expertise of specialists, resources, and the comfortable learning environment. The Open Commons is not regularly scheduled by any group but is available using its own calendaring system. It is the place where one can observe the highest quality of teaching and learning throughout the school. (Loertscher, Koechlin, and Zwaan, 2008, p. 125)

And second,

Experimental Learning Center—the place both physical and virtual where professional development, action research, and experimental programs are being tested, exhibited, and analyzed before going out for widespread adoption in the school. (Loertscher, Koechlin, and Zwaan, 2008, p. 122)

Loertscher and Koechlin's most recent publication to date is two learning commons approach "manuals," with specific companion applications in each manual pertaining to elementary and secondary school focus. These manuals identify "12 important characteristics of the learning commons," with activities, resources, and short videos "designed to be used by librarians, other specialists in the school, administrators, and teachers who are trying to implement the LC concept." Activities have a companion in each other volume, with resources and ideas that differ for age and grade levels (Loertscher and Koechlin, 2015b and c).

In 2013 Professor Loertscher was granted the American Library Association Baber Research Award (American Library Association, 2016), to conduct a study on the impact of co-teaching, planning, and assessment in the school library learning commons on student learning. In an article published about this research, its results, and its implications, two major conclusions show that in the learning commons, "co-teaching makes a major impact on learning" and "allows for experimentation" (Loertscher, 2014). Loertscher declared April 2015 to May 2016 "The Year of the Learning Commons," through designing a project that involves many schools in the United States, Canada, and around the world, as they transition their school libraries to the learning commons approach. With many schools participating, a significant amount of data is being collected relating to ideas, challenges, and successes of learning commons journeys. The schools involved report their progression on an ever-expanding spreadsheet, accessible on the Learning Commons website. The "Year of the Learning Commons" page on the website includes posters, logos, models, and resources that any school is welcome to use in their own websites, presentations, or reports (Loertscher and Koechlin, 2016b). When studying the spreadsheet, readers can see a wide variety of schools at different stages in their journey, which can be used for comparative purposes or as a basis for joining the project.

Teacher-librarians in many schools lead learning commons initiation and development, and many who lead the process document their challenges and successes in school library journals or other forums, such as conference presentations and web spaces. This form of documentation is largely creating a growing body of literature and research on school library learning commons through journal articles, wikis, blog posts, websites, interviews, and papers. Some of this documentation is found in sources such as *Teacher Librarian: The Journal for School Library*

Professionals (Levitov and Kaaland, 2016) or *School Libraries in Canada* (Grose, 2016). The publisher of *Teacher Librarian: The Journal for School Library Professionals* developed a website containing a number of articles originally published in the journal from 2010 to 2014, on the topic of the school library to learning commons approach. These articles provide educators with information relating to a wide variety of differing school contexts and range "from philosophical and foundational explorations of the learning commons concept to first-hand accounts of teacher librarians transforming their traditional libraries into learning commons for the 21st century. Many of the articles are highly illustrated; many provide practical advice, guidance, and instruction at both the micro and macro level" (*Teacher Librarian: The Journal of School Library Professionals*, 2014).

This growing amount of educator research, articles, websites, blogs, online videos, and other media documenting school library learning commons developments provides models for schools to examine, compare to, and learn from—as well as a wealth of on-site practitioner research to replicate. Buffy Hamilton blogs as "The Unquiet Librarian" (Hamilton, 2015) with a wide variety of pedagogical interests and blog entries on "critical literacy, participatory learning and culture, ethnographic studies, critical pedagogy, and writing literacies." The blog "By the Brooks"—Libraries and Learning: Leadership for the School Library Learning Commons, by school library consultant Anita Brooks Kirkland (Brooks Kirkland, 2016) contains current and archived blog posts on school library to learning commons resources and developments. School District Superintendent Chris Kennedy blogs about school library to learning commons, including a blog post on his visits to schools throughout his Vancouver, British Colombia, school division, eager to share their learning commons developments with him (Kennedy, 2015). Students in the University of British Columbia Master of Educational Technology program designed an informative learning commons wiki, highlighting school learning commons history, defining features, educational theories, and remarks on the changing role of the teacher-librarian. On their wiki they include educational theories or strategies that support the learning commons approach, such as "constructivism, collaboration, multimedia learning, connectivism, sociocultural constructivism, distributed cognition, situated cognition/learning, Marzano's instructional strategies, backwards design, differentiated learning, professional learning communities" (McVittie and Duggan, 2014).

Papers, articles, and presentations from Treasure Mountain United States (Loertscher, 2015c) and Treasure Mountain Canada (TMC; 2016) research retreats also depict the context of many diverse schools and how they approach the learning commons transition. Treasure Mountain United States began in 1989 as a research retreat founded and developed by Loertscher and colleagues, to focus on school library research as a "valuable catalyst for school improvement based on contributions and analysis of research in the field and the emergence of the learning commons." Papers from the 2015 retreat, held in Columbus, Ohio (Loertscher, 2015a), include a look at school library to learning commons from the perspective of many school library field experts. Paper topics include co-teaching, statewide initiatives, maker education, shifting to the learning commons perspective, and student learning commons ownership. Treasure Mountain Canada, held every two years since

2010, is an extension of Treasure Mountain United States, and provided impetus to create *Leading Learning: Standards of Practice for School Library Learning Commons in Canada* (Canadian Library Association, 2014b). TMC4, held in Ottawa, Ontario, in 2016, continues to follow the "growing impact" of *Leading Learning*. Papers posted to the TMC site concentrate on implementation efforts of the school library learning commons standards, focusing on co-teaching for deeper learning, innovation for learning, and building a learning community. Both Treasure Mountain United States and Canada research retreat blogs, live streaming, video conference, and archived websites, with papers focused on the learning commons approach, inviting schools to access, learn, and participate even if not attending.

School library associations within countries, states, provinces, and territories, as well as school districts, increasingly produce studies or documents reflecting the shift from school library to the learning commons approach. *Together for Learning: School Libraries and the Emergence of the Learning Commons* (Ontario School Library Association, 2010) is a collaboration between government, the Ontario School Library Association, and school library leaders in response to the forces of change affecting society and schools, "all while ensuring students emerge with the skills they need not only to survive, but to thrive—development of a Learning Commons addresses this challenge" (p. 2). *Together for Learning* defines the learning commons as

> a flexible and responsive approach to helping schools focus on learning collaboratively. It expands the learning experience, taking students and educators into virtual spaces beyond the walls of a school. A Learning Commons is a vibrant, whole-school approach, presenting exciting opportunities for collaboration among teachers, teacher-librarians and students. Within a Learning Commons, new relationships are formed between learners, new technologies are realized and utilized, and both students and educators prepare for the future as they learn new ways to learn. And best of all, as a space traditionally and naturally designed to facilitate people working together, a school's library provides the natural dynamics for developing a Learning Commons. (Ontario School Library Association, 2010, p. 3)

Together for Learning and its subsequent website (Ontario Library Association, 2016) provide educators with a comprehensible blending of learning commons theory and practical implementation tools, making them significant sources to use as a book and web study for educators exploring or implementing the approach. The document discusses the emergence of the learning commons approach, its key components, how it empowers learners, its implementation through a culture of inquiry, personalization of learning, inherent pedagogical shifts, and tactics for evidence-based practice. It details each phase of the inquiry process with cross-curricular learner outcomes, sample activities for either elementary or secondary schools, and a variety of assessment tools for each phase.

The British Columbia Teacher-Librarians Association (BCTLA) document *From School Library to Library Learning Commons: A Pro-Active Model for Educational Change* (Ekdahl and Zubke, 2014) reflects a transformation model based on three years of practitioner research K–12. It focuses on the inquiry question "When and how does a school library become a learning commons?" (p. 5). The document presents a unique chart, illustrating school library to learning commons performance standards metaphorically from "wagon cart" to "sports car" (p. 8). As the authors observe,

> The transformation of a School Library Resource Centre (SLRC) into a Library Learning Commons is an example of one component of how a school or system actively addresses goals of change in response to new kinds of teaching and learning. The goals for change are aligned with evidence from current research and with school, district, and provincial goals. (Ekdahl and Zubke, 2014, p. 5)

The model in this study is established on five components: project, process, program, professional capital (culture of collaboration, practice, and best practices), and product (student success). The document includes checklists for using the model, detailing the components, learning commons student outcomes, and "Points of Inquiry: A Foundational Inquiry Model For Library Learning Commons Programs" (Ekdahl and Zubke, 2014, p. 18). Teacher-librarians in a variety of situations involved in the inquiry share detailed narratives of learning commons implementation, and a list of extensive references is provided.

School districts transitioning to the learning commons approach document and share processes, challenges, and successes. Lexington School District One in Lexington, South Carolina, has been implementing the learning commons philosophy in all of its school libraries since 2011, inspired by David Loertscher. Their experience is described in the chapter "The Learning Commons: From Planning to Practice in a School System in South Carolina, USA," by Kohout and Gavigan, collected in *Global Action on School Library Guidelines* (Schultz-Jones and Oberg, 2015a, pp. 86–92). Lexington School District One defines learning commons as

> both a physical and virtual space staffed by the media specialist, technology integration specialist, instructional coaches, support staff, and trained students. It is a flexible and responsive approach to helping students and educators collaboratively focus on learning. It expands the learning experience, taking students and educators into virtual spaces beyond the walls of the school. The Learning Commons is a vibrant, whole-school approach, presenting exciting opportunities for collaboration among teachers, Media Specialist, Technology Integration Specialist, Instructional Coach, and students. (Lexington School District One, 2015)

The change process in this district has involved using significant collaborative efforts to develop shared vision and understanding of school library to learning commons among all of its schools, and developing rubrics that all of its schools agree on to identify needs in the "physical, virtual, and experimental commons," along with the design and use of rubrics to set professional goals. Kohout and Gavigan reflect that "a successful learning commons is more about creating an active, engaging learner-centered environment than it is about creating the facility itself. The strength of a quality learning commons lies in collaborative learning that occurs between and among the library media specialists, technology integration specialists, classroom teachers, and students" (in Schultz-Jones and Oberg, 2015a, p. 91). No matter the level of support or resources educators access in their learning commons journeys, the authors go on to recommend that educators consider the following advice that they received from David Loertscher:

> Establishing a learning commons in a school can be done with a limited or plentiful amount of resources. Start the programme first, meaning that co-teaching is happening, simultaneous use of physical facilities, the construction of a virtual learning commons and making both students and teachers start to feel like they have ownership of the idea. For those lacking resources, become the world's great scrounge. Ask everyone for help, time, and money to spruce things up. This includes students, teachers, janitors, parents, community organizations and businesses. Lots of folks will pitch in when they feel that the results will make a real difference in teaching and learning. (Quoted in Schultz-Jones and Oberg, 2015, p. 91)

Schools conducting site-based action research examine the literature and research of others, while gathering evidence of their own learning commons approach progression and challenges, to ensure that this forward-thinking pedagogy impacts the student learning goals and outcomes that their school is monitoring. Site-based action research is now widely recognized as a professional development tool "at the center of school improvement" (Reeves, 2008), and guides teacher professional growth throughout the career with its "snowball effect": once an action research cycle is completed, it leads the teacher researcher into further exploration of or connection to the topic—in this case, learning commons. As the development keeps growing, so does the inquiry-based cyclic process of action research. The action research process, in summary, calls for

- refining a topic or issue of current focus within the context of where the school presently is with the approach,
- posing critical questions focused on student learning,
- brainstorming possible information and answers to questions,
- hypothesizing the outcome,
- reviewing pertinent literature in the field and the research of others,
- developing a plan, with goals and outcomes for gathering on-site evidence,
- putting the plan into action,
- analyzing results for patterns and themes to create actions and strategies, and
- reflecting on the results.

Reflecting on the results of research leads to new questions, issues, or directions, re-starting the action research cycle. "Teachers have the support of the teacher-librarian and other specialists in the Learning Commons to help them determine what evidence to gather, how analyze the data, and then how to apply the findings to improve teaching and learning. Becoming a reflective practitioner is a process of discovery" (Loertscher, Koechlin, and Zwaan, 2008, p. 84).

Learning commons action research models and examples are available from the research retreats, journals, books, and websites mentioned above. Reviewing the action research of others is a vital part of getting to know and understand the growing literature and research base of school library to learning commons, and creating a community of learning commons research and researchers. As a school district initiative, the Greater Essex County District School Board in Windsor, Ontario, in partnership with the University of Windsor, has supported teams of educators in collaborative inquiry action research since 2007. The district outlines the collaborative inquiry process in four stages: "framing the problem, collecting evidence, analyzing evidence, celebrating and sharing." The district selects "15 proposals from within-school and between-school teams," and provides teacher release time, a school board consultant and/or university researcher on each team to provide ongoing support, the ability for teams to meet at least four times "to identify inquiry questions related to their teaching practice, to collect and analyze evidence, plan for next steps, and report results," and the the opportunity for sharing of results during a "Learning Fair" where "teams presented their inquiries and findings through posters, display boards, photos and video presentations." Detailed action research reports reflecting most curricular areas and grade levels from this district initiative are available on the district website; many of the projects involve teacher-librarians co-teaching with teacher teams (Greater Essex County District School Board, 2016). Some topics chosen by the district are site-based and contextual; however, the topics are broad enough to inform and inspire other educators in seeking learning commons literature and research to review, or to provide ideas for replicating or conducting their own research on similar topics of interest or concern. For instance, projects from the district's 2014–15 reports include the following:

- Eliciting collaboration between the teacher librarian and classroom teacher to create an inviting, accessible learning commons space and improve student information literacy skills
- Investigating the impact of Teacher Librarian/Teacher collaboration on student achievement
- Changing the ways in which students engage in the research process
- Impacting teaching practice through collaboration between homeroom teachers and teacher librarians

The district's 2010–2011 report focuses exclusively on teacher-librarian action research, with topics such as

- How can the teacher librarian who is also the vice-principal support classroom teachers?
- Will the integration of technology into projects developed and implemented in collaboration with the teacher librarian increase teacher confidence and willingness to integrate technology into future lessons and will this use of technology increase student engagement?

(Greater Essex County District School Board, 2016)

The developing literature and teacher research on the learning commons approach serves as impetus for conversation and building shared understanding, ideas, and ongoing action planning; enlightens action research; and provides a base for schools to explore, implement, or take the WSLLC to the next level.

Chapter 7

SELECTED LEARNING COMMONS LITERATURE AND RESEARCH WITH STRATEGIES

As professional educators, School Librarians should exemplify the vision for being life-long learners.... Who better to facilitate book studies and action research projects leading to professional development for teachers than the media specialist? (Brown, Dotson, and Yontz, 2011, pp. 56, 60)

Teacher-librarians, principals, and WSLLC steering teams lead faculties in building thoughtful shared understanding of the "whys" and "hows" involved in implementing a learning commons approach, through sharing and interacting with key literature in the field and student impact research studies. They continue to update the faculty on new resources and developments. Educators apply this knowledge and findings to ongoing learning commons approach practice and by conducting either formal or informal action research.

As learning commons leaders share key literature and research, engage faculty in interacting with it, and gather thoughts and ideas to enable action planning, inevitably the issue of funding surfaces in discussion or response. Some faculty members think the school cannot fiscally afford to move into the approach, either in reference to a physical "makeover" of the school library, or in the ability to hire a teacher-librarian or learning commons lead teacher. A key message to remember when the topic of funding arises is that the learning commons transformation can begin with little funding or plenty of funding; the most important thing is the pedagogical focus on impacting student learning through collaborative planning, teaching, and assessing of curriculum based on collective analysis of student data.

Funding for enhancements and resources needed or desired is planned along the way as the faculty and community engage in the transformation, develop outcome-based budgets, and apply for grants or district initiative programs. Many quality resources approved for students—such as reference works, journals, and e-books—are accessible in digital format and available at no cost to schools through state or provincial library network licensing. These include formats for students requiring visual, auditory, tactile, or other learning supports. Once educators understand and start to see how learning commons pedagogy impacts student learning and can begin with little or no cost, students, parents, and partnerships can help find ways to fund future spaces and resources.

Funding for a teacher-librarian or lead learning commons teacher is more challenging, as most schools are allocated staffing ratios from the district via state, provincial, or territorial per-student funding allocations. There are many creative ways "to ensure learners have the best professional support and expertise possible in their library learning commons." A list of creative scenarios from *Leading Learning: Standards of Practice for School Library Learning Commons in Canada* (Canadian Library Association, 2014b, p. 36) helps schools look at various ways to provide learning commons professional support and create their own working scenarios. Some ideas to accomplish this include hiring a part-time teacher-librarian or learning commons lead teacher who would share the role with other school specialist teachers, such as reading or technology teachers, in collaboration with the classroom teachers. Or librarians, library technicians, and learning commons lead teachers working in partnership with a travelling or virtual teacher librarian. A number of schools share "a virtual teacher-librarian supporting e-learning or blended learning experiences linked to online learning environments via a Virtual Learning Commons" (CLA, 2014b, p. 36). As schools begin or continue to explore learning commons literature and research, they continually learn about or develop creative solutions to ongoing concerns and adapt contextual situations to best-practice focus on impacting student learning with professional support. The following selected key literature and research sources and strategies enable facilitation of key learning commons literature and resources. Use additional resources for the strategies as pertinent.

WSLLC Reading and Research Resource 1:

"Flip This Library: School Libraries Need a Revolution" (Loertscher, 2008)

WSLLC Reading and Research Strategy 1:

Introducing the WSLLC—Gathering Thoughts

When school and school library leaders begin to explore the learning commons approach, they often discover that very few other educators on the faculty have familiarity with the school library to learning commons movement or view it as a whole school approach. Often the initiative to explore the approach comes from the teacher-librarian and/or other school library personnel; sometimes the school district or principal initiates the approach. Faculty members wonder why there is a need to transform the school library to a learning commons, especially as a whole school approach. To introduce the approach and its "hows and whys," have principals or teacher-librarians select a readable, distinct article, such as the classic pioneering article "Flip This Library: School Libraries Need a Revolution" (Loertscher, 2008). This particular article inspires educators to learn about and explore the transformation of school libraries to learning commons when shared during staff meetings or other professional learning events. In this article, one of Loertscher's earliest on shifting to the learning commons perspective, Loertscher challenges schools to transform their libraries in "revolution" rather than evolution. The article provides the foundational school library learning commons philosophy and descriptors, as well as outlining what various educators in schools do in their roles to enact the "flip" from school library to learning commons. The "flip" focuses on the "client (student) based approach" and answers some of the "can'ts" and "won't happens" that arise in discussions. Loertscher includes a diagrammatic chart, "The Paradigm Flip" (Loertscher, 2008, p. 48), illustrating school library to learning commons changes.

Have the principal, teacher-librarian, or steering team deciding to use the article request that educators pre-read it prior to an upcoming meeting or professional development activity, or provide time at the meeting to read it, depending on what works best with the particular faculty. Once read, lead a discussion focused on the school using the headings of "The Paradigm Flip" chart stems from the article:

- Where we are
- Where we need to go
- Now let's get even more radical …

(Loertscher, 2008, p. 48)

Read and discuss the article stems in small groups or online, to gather information. Post large sheets of chart paper depicting the stems and responses for a determined period of time in the school professional area, ideally located in the physical and virtual commons, so that faculty can view, consider, add to, and build on responses. The responses and comments will inform and alert the principal, teacher-librarian, or steering team with information to decide what literature or actions to next present.

WSLLC Reading and Research Resource 2:

The New Learning Commons: Where Learners Win! Reinventing School Libraries and Computer Labs, 2nd Ed. (Loertscher, Koechlin, and Zwaan, 2011b)

WSLLC Reading and Research Strategy 2:

Book Study—Make It Appetizing!

What do key experts in the learning commons field say about transforming school libraries to the learning commons approach? Schools, school districts, states, provinces or territories, and countries, academic school library researchers, or graduate students, often begin the exploration of learning commons pedagogy through studying and applying strategies from the work and publications of Loertscher, Koechlin, and Zwaan, frequently with the resource *The New Learning Commons: Where Learners Win! Reinventing School Libraries and Computer Labs, 2nd Ed.* (Loertscher, Koechlin, and Zwaan, 2011b). Have teacher-librarians or steering teams facilitate a book study of this key resource, or others by the authors and their collaborators, by organizing monthly "appetizer" meetings after school. Participants enjoy snacks and conversation, and provide thoughts and ideas as they study chapters or sections of the book planned for each meeting.

Use the book study prompts: What do we already know from this chapter(s)? What did we learn from it? What do we question or want to know more about? Summarize and record responses for future planning. Have participants record response summaries on "sticky" notes and paste them onto chart paper, or digitally on a Google doc spreadsheet with a smart board, to observe comments as they build, using virtual "sticky notes" with a tool such as iBrainstorm (Universal Mind, 2012). Have learning commons leaders and teams provide and gain information for next steps on a timely basis and plan what is needed for going forward. Continue book studies with related titles, authored by key experts.

WSLLC Reading and Research Resource 3:

learningcommons (Loertscher and Koechlin, 2016a)
and/or
National Project: National Standards for School Libraries in Canada Project (Voices for School Libraries Network, 2016)

WSLLC Reading and Research Strategy 3:
Conduct a Website Study with "Cookies"

Engage the faculty in a website study led by the principal, teacher-librarian, or steering team, to explore the learning commons approach. The LearningCommons website, created by experts Loertscher and Koechlin as a companion to their foundational learning commons books, can be studied with the books or independently. The site is organized into "physical learning commons, virtual learning commons, and knowledge building centers" sections, along with resources, news, tools, and strategies. The *National Project: National Standards for School Libraries in Canada Project* site (Voices for School Libraries Network, 2016) documents the process of creating new national school library learning commons standards and is updated on a regular basis by Koechlin. Its "Moving Forward" page contains current information regarding learning commons implementation, articles, presentations, videos, and other developments that benefit steering team members to study together, to discover resources of interest, or to use with the entire staff in understanding and advancing the approach.

Each month at a regular staff meeting or other dedicated professional learning time, have members from the steering team or volunteers from the faculty take turns showcasing a page or part of the website. Call it "cookie time," and share a plate of cookies to enjoy along with the presentation. The presenter chooses a key link or links to share, such as a video recommended on the page that they present. Ask participants as they leave the session to write at least one "take-away" idea they think enhances learning commons development at the school from that day's web page presentation on large, brightly colored sticky notes or even paper "cookies," and post as "Web Study Think-Abouts."

WSLLC Reading and Research Resource 4:

"By the Brooks"—Libraries and Learning: Leadership for the School Library Learning Commons (Brooks Kirkland, 2016)

WSLLC Reading and Research Strategy 4:

Blog Study

One venue for discovering key literature on the learning commons is through the increase of blogs written by experts in the field and school-based practitioners. "By the Brooks"—Libraries and Learning: Leadership for the School Library Learning Commons (Brooks Kirkland, 2016), written by school library learning commons consultant Anita Brooks Kirkland, focuses largely on the shift from school library to learning commons. This blog is archived from 2012 and updated regularly with information, news, ideas, and posts specifically related to learning commons developments. Have the principal, teacher-librarian, or steering team preview the blog's home page, tags, and categories, and select key links they feel pertain to their context that they would like to share when showcasing this or any other blog to the faculty. Use the chart on page 94 to explore the blog and record comments for discussion and sharing. Participants and facilitators can decide whether they wish to post comments to the actual blog.

WSLLC Reading and Research Resource 5:

Leading Learning Bibliography (Canadian Library Association, 2014a)

WSLLC Reading and Research Strategy 5:

Color-Coordinating Literature and Research

An extensive bibliography (Canadian Library Association, 2014a) supports *Leading Learning: Standards of Practice for School Library Learning Commons in Canada* (Canadian Library Association, 2014b) and contains many key resources on the school library to learning commons approach. These resources are referenced

WSLLC Blog Study Chart (Sample)

Blog Name/Link: E.g., "By the Brooks" http://www. bythebrooks.ca/	Current Post on the Blog: "Teacher-Librarian 2.0"	Selected Tag: "Knowledge Building Centers"	Selected Category Post: "Guided Inquiry"	Leave a Comment(s) on Current or Selected Post
I agree with …				
I learned …				
I would debate …				
I would like to learn more about …				

WSLLC Blog Study Chart

Blog Name/Link:	Current Post on the Blog:	Selected Tag:	Selected Category Post:	Leave a Comment(s) on Current or Selected Post
I agree with …				
I learned …				
I would debate …				
I would like to learn more about …				

or highlighted throughout the standards document itself, most notably in the "See it in Action" example descriptions. As noted there are five inter-connecting standards in *Leading Learning*, developed to support a whole school learning commons approach. These five standards are colored and symbolic rather than numbered, so as not to appear hierarchical, with schools being at different points in each of the standard phases and indicators—leading in some, emerging in others. The work of an effective learning commons is framed when these core standards of practice weave together to generate dynamic learning.

Approach interacting with the literature and research presented in an extensive bibliography such as this by having facilitators (the principal, teacher-librarian, and/or steering team) divide the faculty into groups in this case based on the colors of the standards—red, green, orange, blue, and purple—with a leader or leaders from the steering team facilitating each group. Wear t-shirts or hats in the standard color, or use felt pens, sticky notes, font color, paper, etc., in the standard color to record responses and ideas. Each group is responsible to study and present to the faculty pertinent literature or resources discovered in their standard's section, over a series of meetings or professional learning days. Groups decide on one or two contextually appropriate examples or sources to share, and collect responses from the faculty regarding applicability to or ideas for their school. Have groups suggest "action examples" from the school that also illustrate the standard. Following presentations by all groups, discuss which standard concept the faculty desires more reading or information about, especially in terms of applicability to their school and the learning commons approach.

WSLLC Reading and Research Resource 6:

"Divine Design: How to Create the 21st-Century School Library of Your Dreams" (Sullivan, 2011a)
and
"Transforming Library Spaces" (Brooks Kirkland, 2013)

WSLLC Reading and Research Strategy 6:

Participatory Learning "Architects"

The learning commons approach is supported by the collective design of rich physical and virtual learning environments that work in tandem to meet the co-determined needs of the students. These collaborative spaces include multiple modalities of effective instructional design and student learning, to provide seamless access for all students to exemplary resource collections in all formats and enhance learning experiences. The book *The Third Teacher* (OWP/P Architects, VS Furniture, and Bruce Mau Design, 2010) and its accompanying website (Cannon Design, 2016) present collaborations by architects and designers in the importance of rethinking the actual "environment as an essential element of learning." Whether educators explore or are immersed in the learning commons approach, the physical environment is one of the first and ongoing components schools work on as a key visual representation and learning space for the approach in practice.

Engage the faculty in preparing small group or partner "presentations" to imagine or re-imagine the school physical library spaces for a learning commons approach. Have the principal, teacher-librarian, or members of the steering team request that faculty members consider "wishes and dreams" for the physical learning commons based on the current physical space of the school library. Do this activity over a series of staff meetings or professional learning activity events in the current school library space. Have participants assume they are groups or pairs of "architects" from various different architectural firms, and have them create a name for their "firm."

To prepare a dream version of the physical learning commons, have participants read "Divine Design: How to Create the 21st-Century School Library of Your Dreams" (Sullivan, 2011a) and "Transforming Library Spaces" (Brooks Kirkland, 2013). There are many resources available on school library/learning commons design, but begin by using one or two sources such as the ones mentioned in this strategy, and let the groups or teams imagine what they think is possible for their school site and students. Request that they "think big," as well as letting them know that they are to include up to five "manageable" first steps from their ideas. To share, have participants choose a medium of their preference—drawings, lists, Lego models, etc.—whatever materials are handily available. Encourage wishing, dreaming, and designing possibilities for the learning commons; however, have each "firm" ensure that their ideas meet the following criteria:

- Spaces for collaboration, hands-on learning, presentations, communication, creativity
- Spaces to support individual, small group, and whole class activities
- Flexible spaces easy to change dependent on activity
- Engaging spaces for students and teachers
- Spaces accessible for all students
- Inclusive resource collection, with many varied formats
- Other criteria pertinent to own context

Share the presentations, celebrating the ideas and pointing out commonalities that emerge among the "firms," as well as agreeing on doable first steps.

WSLLC Reading and Research Resource 7:

Together for Learning (Ontario Library Association, 2016)

WSLLC Reading and Research Strategy 7:

Virtual Scavenger Hunt

The *Together for Learning* document is a unique collaboration between a school library association and government ministry of education. It is one of the first such documents (originally published in 2010) to focus distinctly on the emergence

Together for Learning*: Virtual Scavenger Hunt

Locate and Read	Reflect	Apply
Under "T4L Vision Document" ⇓	One to three things I learned from reading this section	Idea(s) to use at my school for WSLLC
1. Definition of Learning Commons		
2. The New Learner		
3. Learning Partnerships		
4. Role of Differentiated Instruction		
5. Learning to Learn		
6. Making the Learning Commons Happen		
7. Phases of Inquiry		
8. The Importance of Individual Growth		
9. Personal Learning Networks		
10. Multiple Literacies		
Under "Implementation" ⇓		
11. Learning Commons Team		
12. Collaborative Learning and Teaching		
13. School Improvement		
14. Learning to Learn Ideas		
15. Reading Engagement Ideas		
Under "Supporting You" ⇓		
16. Supporting Principals		
17. Supporting All Teachers		
Under "Links"—Choose one and explore it ⇓		
18.		
Bonus Points! Choose two topics not on this list that interest you ⇓		
19.		
20.		

* www.togetherforlearning.ca

of the learning commons. Its accompanying website (Ontario Library Association, 2016) is continually updated and provides educators with a clear blending of learning commons theory and practical tools, with many things to learn about learning commons and its implementation, both in the document and on the site. The following "virtual scavenger hunt" is designed to take educators through this particular website, but one can use the "scavenger hunt" technique to explore other sites, wikis, or blogs. Do this activity independently to build background knowledge on the shift from school library to learning commons, or as a faculty or network activity over time, arranging to meet during a staff meeting, professional event, or network meeting, to discuss what is discovered about learning commons from the source and how this applies to your context. If the activity is done collectively, award a small prize such as a bookmark to the first participant to complete the scavenger hunt, or the one(s) with the most completed stems. Use the chart on page 98 as a guide for the activity.

WSLLC Reading and Research Resource 8:

"School Library Research Summarized: A Graduate Class Project" (Kachel and Graduate Students of LSC 5530, Mansfield University, 2013)

WSLLC Reading and Research Strategy 8:

Research Poster Art

A vast and growing amount of educational research shows quality school libraries with teacher-librarians provide advantages to student learning, no matter the demographics or level of parental education. Action researchers conduct inquiries applicable to the learning commons approach, postulating that with a whole school approach to collaborative planning, teaching, and assessment based on student data, student learning advantages will continue to rise. As schools move into the approach, educators study background knowledge relating to educational research in school libraries and learning commons, and summaries of the research are helpful. A concise summary of school library impact research is found in "School Library Research Summarized: A Graduate Class Project" (Kachel and Graduate Students of LSC 5530, Mansfield University, 2013), compiled by School Library Advocacy and Leadership instructor Kachel and graduate students of the School Library and Information Technologies Graduate Program, Mansfield University, Mansfield, PA. Have participants read the summary, noting whether their state is included in the study summary, and generate ideas or observations applicable to the school from the research. Create posters highlighting their ideas and observations, with the heading "School Library Research Summary and [name of] School." Provide felt pens, colored pencils, discarded magazines, or other materials to illustrate, collage, and enliven the posters. Share the posters orally, then scan and post onto the school virtual learning commons as pertinent. Use the chart on page 100 to guide the activity.

WSLLC Research Poster Art

"School Library Impact Studies: The Major Findings from the Past Ten Years" (Kachel, 2013)	Two Things Learned from the Research Summary	Related School Observations	Ideas for Applying Research to Develop Our WSLLC
STAFFING			
COLLABORATION			
INSTRUCTION			
SCHEDULING			
ACCESS			
TECHNOLOGY			
COLLECTIONS			
BUDGET			
PROFESSIONAL DEVELOPMENT			
ACHIEVEMENT GAP			

> **WSLLC Reading and Research Resource 9:**
>
> Treasure Mountain Research Retreat (Loertscher, 2015c)
> and
> Treasure Mountain Canada (Treasure Mountain Canada, 2016)
>
> **WSLLC Reading and Research Strategy 9:**
>
> Hold a "Mini Treasure Mountain"

A great deal can be learned from examining and replicating the research of others, both formal and informal, and a growing body of sources makes this possible and available for educators, in relation to transforming school libraries to the learning commons approach. Papers and projects shared at the "Treasure Mountain" school library learning commons retreats provide extensive samples of school-based action research and implementation strategies developing about the learning commons approach. As previously noted, Treasure Mountain research retreats originated in the United States with David Loertscher in 1989, to provide researchers in the field of "school library media studies" an opportunity to share their research, gather ideas, and interact with practitioners "in the field." The retreats grew to embrace developments in school library to the learning commons movement. The Treasure Mountain retreats usually open with a keynote speaker who is an expert in the field, followed by breakout sessions where paper writers present a synopsis of their research or project in fifteen- or twenty-minute segments, followed by five or ten minutes for questions or discussion about the paper or project being presented. Paper writers move on to present to a second and third group within the hour. Depending on the number of participants or papers, the process may be repeated again in the day. Some experts in the field or presenters not physically in attendance for the retreat may join in to present virtually. The event concludes with an overall synthesizing activity to unite the retreat learning.

Create a "Mini Treasure Mountain" in your school, network, or district. Have WSLLC leaders or teams select papers or projects found online from the United States or Canadian research retreats, or from other learning commons literature or research sources that they feel best suit their context. In addition, invite members of your school, network, or district to write brief papers or project summaries, discussing their experiences with exploring or developing the approach. Organize a professional day presenting papers or articles from Treasure Mountain or school members to small groups. Invite a keynote speaker, either in person or virtually, to enhance the day, or have the facilitators kick off the day with a presentation they create for their school or district, adapted from sources such as the LearningCommons website (Loertscher and Koechlin, 2016), which includes a web page with presentations to use or adapt. Participants listen to literature, research, or projects pertaining to developing the learning commons approach, in small groups throughout the day, and reconvene to synthesize the learning through an activity such as collaboratively writing an acrostic poem by composing a sentence or two for the letters "WSLLC" and sharing and posting the poems. Have each individual leave the session by writing out one key takeaway point from the retreat on colorful paper strips provided, to also post, share, and use for planning. If school or district members compose their own papers, compile an anthology and encourage writers to think about sharing a paper or project at the next TMC United States or Canada retreat.

WSLLC Reading and Research Resource 10:

"Year of the Learning Commons" (Loertscher and Koechlin, 2016b)

WSLLC Reading and Research Strategy 10:

Join In—Take Away!

Dr. David Loertscher declared April 2015 to May 2016 as "The Year of the Learning Commons!" through a project in the United States, in Canada, and around the world, toward the building of a global learning commons community of practice. In the project, schools participate and follow the work of other schools developing and documenting their school library to learning commons transition. The "Year of the Learning Commons" web page (Loertscher and Koechlin, 2016b) includes posters, logos, and other resources ("take-aways") for schools to use on websites, in presentations, and in school reports. The "School Learning Commons International Registry" spreadsheet provides short descriptions of the variety of participating schools implementing the learning commons approach, as well as contact information. More detailed information is found on a second spreadsheet, where participants contribute to and update a survey with questions regarding the state of their physical and virtual learning commons and what they view in their schools as "the most important contributions of the LC to teaching and learning."

Study the project and decide to join in, contribute, and learn from the work of others in the various stages of learning commons development. Prior to joining in, have teacher-librarians, lead learning commons teachers, or steering teams work with the faculty to prepare information to share, relating to the four key questions on the spreadsheet, as applicable to their school context. You can still use the questions to discuss your learning commons as a faculty if you decide not to join the project.

1. What is the state of your learning commons? (i.e., "making good progress, some progress, slight progress")
2. What are the most important contributions of the learning commons to teaching and learning?
3. What contributions to learning is the physical space of the learning commons making?
4. What is the current state of the Virtual Learning Commons?

Once educators process these four questions, and any other questions they wish to add, study the "Year of the Learning Commons" spreadsheet on the website, to learn from and compare how other schools in the project responded. List up to five new ideas or next steps to "take away" from the experiences of others in the project. Whether the faculty chooses to join the project or not, study the results from participants who represent a variety of diverse contexts. Consider joining other schools in your neighborhood, district, or community to create a "local spreadsheet" of learning commons development. Use the following chart to guide the activity.

"Year of the Learning Commons": Join In—Take Away!

"Year of the Learning Commons" Survey Questions (Loertscher and Koechlin, 2016b)	Observations from Survey Participant Comments	"Take-Aways": New Ideas or Next Steps
What is the state of your learning commons?		
What are the most important contributions of the LC to teaching and learning?		
What contributions to learning is the physical space of the LC making?		
What is the current state of the Virtual Learning Commons?		

WSLLC Reading and Research Resource 11:
Conducting Action Research to Evaluate Your School Library (Sykes, 2013)

WSLLC Reading and Research Strategy 11:
Study Your Own School

Douglas Reeves writes about "action research at the center of school improvement" (Reeves, 2008). School principals ensure on-site action research; documentation of the learning commons approach is encouraged, enabled, and shared. In the book *Conducting Action Research to Evaluate Your School Library* (Sykes, 2013), I explore how teacher librarians or learning commons lead teachers and teams can get directly involved with the action research process in their own schools. This process facilitates accountability for learning in the actions and plans created to impact student learning and benefit professional growth, by gathering on-site evidence and analyzing results. Here are some ideas for action research in areas of interest to schools in their learning commons journeys:

- Finding Time for Research
- Emergence of the Learning Commons

- Reading (Breadth and Depth in Children's Literature)
- Student Achievement Data
- Creating a School-Wide Student Information Literacy Learning Continuum via Collaborative Planning and Teaching
- Incorporating New and Emerging Technology in Learning
- Interdisciplinary Learning
- Advocacy

(Sykes, 2013, pp. 77–96)

Many schools select similar ideas for learning commons action research or have other issues and topics relating to their current context.

Studying one's own school provides a cycle to develop around knowing, sustaining, and reflecting on goal-setting for implementation and sustainability of an initiative such as learning commons. A simple way to look at the action research process in summary is as follows:

- Consider your present program and the needs of learners.
- Review (applicable) standards of practice (e.g., AASL, Common Core, CLA).
- Identify a target for improvement.
- Develop questions to guide your work.
- Imagine how you might achieve your target.
- Investigate what others have tried and develop your own plan.
- Try it out, adjust strategies if necessary and keep track of your evidence.
- Analyze and interpret your results.
- Prepare a summary report and share.
- Apply your findings to school wide improvement.
- Select another target …

(Koechlin and Sykes, 2014)

As the teacher-librarian, learning commons lead teacher, or steering team initiate action research, use these basic questions to provide insight into a learning commons action research project.

- What is working?
- What isn't?
- What will we do next?
- What insights do others offer us?

All educators in the faculty play important parts in the action research process. The chart on the following page outlines some of the roles, reasons, and strategies for educators' engagement in the WSLLC action research. Add to the chart depending on your context.

Action Research—Roles and Reasons

Educator Role	Why Engage in WSLLC Site-Based Action Research?	Strategies to Enable WSLLC Site-Based Action Research	WSLLC Site-Based Action Research Role Interactions
Principal	- contributes to the whole school development plan and shows how WSLLC is impacting student and teacher learning - is a profound professional learning opportunity - use data collected to plan next steps for WSLLC and school development plan	- discuss action research potential and possibilities and offer assistance when meeting with teacher-librarians and teachers about professional growth plans - ensure that action research aligns with the school plan and district goals - take an active interest in following the action research stages as they unfold, and offer coaching and guidance - initiate action research	- mentor fellow administrators and action researchers in how to support and guide action research
*Other School Administrators	- demonstrates how WSLLC incorporates best instructional practice methodology - demonstrates student and teacher learning growth and future learning needs for school plan infusing WSLLC	- be part of the action research team - initiate the action research - provide resources for action research	- support the principal's direction and leadership for WSLLC action research - support and/or collaborate with the teacher-librarian and/or other WSLLC action researchers
Teacher-Librarian	- further own knowledge regarding WSLLC and student impact - discover what principal, teacher, teacher-librarian colleagues want to learn about or increase practice in for the WSLLC approach - provide insight into contextual issues	- initiate project based on issue or idea - brainstorm with and continually inform principal to refine research - discover what support is available in the school and district for the proposed research	- explicate how the research informs others of the centrality of the teacher-librarian's practice throughout the school - further inform the co-planning, teaching, and assessing with teachers - enable mentoring and involving other teachers in the research
Teachers	- contribute to the understanding of the impact of co-teaching on teacher practice and student learning - gain insight into contextual issues - plan for future learning experiences	- participate in research via co-teaching segment with the teacher-librarian	- demonstrate heightened interconnectedness of practice and disciplines - mentor and be mentored through the process

* Vice principal, department heads, etc.

Part IV

COMMUNITY AND WSLLC

Chapter 8

ENGAGING COMMUNITY

In an organic, living community information and ideas flow freely through the entire network, and the diversity of interpretations and learning styles—even the diversity of mistakes—will enrich the entire community. (Capra, 1996)

Engaging the school community in a learning approach such as the WSLLC initiative encompasses school-based, local, and global factions, all overseen by the principal. Students and staff members build understanding, share ownership, and actively involve themselves in the initiative, ideally facilitated and guided through professional learning teams such as a WSLLC steering team led by a teacher-librarian. Moving out into the local community, parent engagement occurs in many different ways to support such initiatives and strengthen the impact of the approach, as parents learn about how such an initiative enhances their children's learning. More globally, initiatives such as the learning commons approach benefit from educators reaching out to communicate to and involve the immediate community neighborhood, school partnerships, the school district and its various services, the broader municipality, other libraries, and the provisions and connections provided by virtual environments. Engaging community situates the learning commons as a whole school community approach and responsibility. The important characteristic of engaging the learning community with the learning commons is inclusivity, recognizing that "Everyone is a learner; everyone is a teacher working collaboratively toward excellence" (Canadian Library Association, 2014b, p. 5). The learning community members and associates plan and work together to implement and sustain the approach, supporting and mentoring each other in a knowledge-building framework that aspires to develop wisdom and continual growth in learning. Without inclusively engaging the many facets of community, the approach will not easily come to fruition, be sustained, or continue to grow.

Engage the community to explore, implement, and sustain the learning commons approach through forming a WSLLC steering team: "Leadership in the Learning Commons is team-based rather than centralized in a single individual. Each school begins with the functions desirable in the Learning Commons and then organizes various leadership teams to carry out those program elements" (Loertscher, Koechlin, and Zwaan, 2011b, p. 147). Ensure that the steering team's focus is on collaborative instructional design to impact co-determined student learning needs from student assessment data. Each member of the steering team contributes in various ways applicable to their roles and responsibilities. The concept of such leadership teams in schools—"collaborative teams that work interdependently to achieve common goals"—is rooted in the professional learning community movement, shown as one of the most successful sustainable school improvement initiatives of the past few decades (Eaker, Dufour, and Dufour, 2002, p. 3). The learning commons steering team approach is congruent with the movement's professional learning community tenets and leadership practices in "developing high performing ... collaborative teams that work interdependently to achieve common goals" (DuFour, DuFour, Eaker and Karhnek, 2004, pp. 3, 5).

Well-functioning steering teams initially engage the community through sharing and discussing information and background relating to the approach, and outline why the school is developing this approach and what it encompasses. The teams keep all community members up-to-date on events and progress, through various modes and channels of communication, and celebrate successes with the community along the way. The teams mentor and replace team members as they come and go, to increase the sustainability of the approach. Successful steering teams facilitate methods and strategies that welcome community participation in a variety and number of inclusive ways, strategizing to involve all students and staff members on a continual basis, and striving to keep the broader community members informed, involved, and participating frequently. Effective steering teams focus their efforts and key messages on enhancing student success by meeting curricular mandate through accountability for learning processes and practices founded on co-determined, contextually based student needs. The teams share, discuss, and follow literature and research that pertains to the approach, and formally or informally conduct on-site action research to affirm the transformational work. The team guides the learning community in the design of rich physical and virtual learning spaces that support collaboration in instructional design and co-teaching. The members of an ideal learning commons approach steering team include the principal and other school administrator(s), teacher-librarian (or appointed learning commons lead teacher, if the school does not have a teacher-librarian), library technician and other library staff members, teacher(s), student(s), and parent(s). Teams also include additional community members as contextually fitting, such as a librarian from the nearby public library branch.

What does each steering team member offer, in implementing the approach? The support, leadership, and guidance of the principal is critical in engaging the community in the initiative and embedding it within the school development planning process. The principal's membership and representation on the steering team is essential to effectively involve the whole school in the approach, as the principal develops and outlines expectations for all faculty members in moving forward, to ensure that all students equally benefit: "At the school level, the principal is key in establishing and encouraging working partnerships among staff and students. The principal must provide the climate for co-operation, experimentation and growth. The Learning Commons has great potential, but only when everyone participates" (Ontario School Library Association, 2010, p. 40). In some schools, the principal initiates the approach and forms the steering team. The principal is foremost in engaging the broader community, such as in this example from an elementary school in Texas, where the principal envisioned transforming the school library to a learning commons:

> [The principal] had many conversations with my team leaders, teachers, students, PTA, parents, local businesses, churches, and other schools. The conversations were about what we wanted in our LC, in essence: What activities/experiences would be most beneficial for our students? The list included: Makerspace, green screen video, Lego robotics, Makey Makey, collaboration center, Little Bits, Hexbugs, question board, research lab, cardboard creation, reverse engineering, iPad tech-bar, coding, iMovie center, drama/puppet area, and more. We knew what we wanted, the dream was set, our PTA was on board, but we needed money and community support… With the PTA's support…our teachers, community, and parents rose to the occasion, and raised enough money to redesign and furnish our Learning Commons. Additionally, Chase Oaks Church worked with the city to help collect used iPads and smart phones to be donated to our school. (Steele, 2015, pp. 15–16)

If the principal isn't able to attend each steering meeting or learning commons event, they request representation from the vice principal or another administrator, to attend on his or her behalf. If the principal is teaching classes, they model the approach by collaboratively planning, teaching, and assessing instruction with the teacher-librarian and/or other teachers. If not teaching classes, the principal and other school administrators remain visible in learning commons spaces, activities, and approaches, enable flexible scheduling, and plan and participate when possible as another teacher in various co-teaching experiences, to once again model collaboration in instructional design and pedagogical leadership. By being part of collaborative learning and teaching, the principal gains invaluable firsthand insight into the learning needs of many of the students and the thinking behind the planning processes and practices of the teachers involved, coaching and mentoring teachers while working side by side with them and the students. The principal gains greater insight into leading, encouraging, and enabling specific professional development activities for further growth and resilience.

In schools with a teacher-librarian—certificated teachers with graduate study in school librarianship—the teacher-librarian most likely forms and leads the steering team, with the support and involvement of the principal and other administrators, and organizes and provides professional development for the initiative. A learning commons lead teacher also leads steering teams, and is sometimes a teacher-librarian in training or aspiring to state certification, following school librarianship education and licensing information on the American Association of School Librarians website (American Association of School Librarians, 2016d). A learning commons lead teacher is a teacher assigned or appointed to responsibility for the school library learning commons, such as a teacher in the school who displays interest in pursuing teacher-librarianship and the instructional leadership component—perhaps an English teacher or technology teacher—or another school administrator, such as the vice principal. In any event, one person cannot do it all. As pointed out earlier in this book, often when the teacher-librarian or learning commons lead teacher leaves, the learning commons development slows down or regresses. For the approach to thrive, everyone in the school shares ownership, and the steering team includes representation from all facets of the learning community.

Engaging the community in the school library has always been paramount to the role of a teacher-librarian, and this continues as school libraries transform into the learning commons approach. Like other librarians, teacher-librarians find that their role keeps evolving and changing as the roles of libraries evolve and change, yet the core competencies of the effective teacher-librarian from best-practice literature remain crucial. Effective teacher-librarian core competencies important to the learning commons approach include "continuous learners, learning leader experts in current learning theory, staff developers, guides/mediators/facilitators of information and multi-literacy, and collaborative practitioners" (Association for Teacher-Librarianship in Canada, and Canadian School Library Association, 1997). Effective teacher-librarians in the learning commons approach are first and foremost teaching partners who bring pedagogical, information, and library expertise to collaborative instructional design, to engage students and teachers in participatory learning. Effective teacher-librarians bring resident expertise in engaging the community in technology for learning:

> Once seen as the gatekeepers of knowledge who resided in the warehouse called the library, teacher-librarians today must adapt to the changing environment brought on by the ever expanding digital world and emerging technologies and become leaders in integrating technology into the learning environment. That environment may at times take them out of the library and into the classroom, where their expertise in research, and in developing inquiry-based projects can be utilized.... (McVittie and Duggan, 2014)

Many teacher-librarians have specialized master's degrees in education, founded on the belief "that teacher-librarians are learning specialists in schools and that a Master of Education degree provides the leadership skills necessary to take on this important role." Teachers specializing in teacher-librarianship "explore leadership in inquiry, literacies, technology, and resources" to "become part of a community with other teachers and teacher-librarians across the country" (University of Alberta, 2016). Teacher-librarian communities are found through district, state, and national networks and organizations, as well as within neighboring or feeder schools, providing teacher-librarians with mentorship and professional learning opportunities to support leading the learning commons, with steering teams engaging the community, and continually reinforcing the focus on co-designing, planning, teaching, and assessing of instruction based on student context. In schools without teacher-librarians, the learning commons lead teacher strives to fulfill aspects of this role, in engaging the steering team and the community.

Teachers come to learning commons pedagogy and steering teams with a wide range of experiences and knowledge in relation to school libraries, libraries in general, learning commons, and collaborative planning, teaching, and assessment. Some teachers have experience working in schools with effective school library programs and have co-taught with teacher-librarians; other teachers have some team-teaching experience with another teacher; and others have little or no experience in collaborative instructional design and practice and how it benefits both students and teachers. Teachers and teacher representatives who volunteer to be on the steering team ensure that learning commons designing and planning meets the needs of their students, as collectively determined in school development student data analysis. They become knowledgeable about print and digital resources, to make certain that learning commons collections and spaces are wholly accessible for all student learning needs.

Most steering teams have at least one to two teacher representatives, depending on the size and context of the school. In an elementary school, often there is one teacher from each division, primary and upper elementary. In a secondary school, each grade or certain departments may provide a representative. In many cases, teachers familiar and comfortable with effective school libraries, or who have had positive experience with co-teaching, will be the teachers who volunteer as teacher representatives for the steering teams. In other cases, teacher representatives become inspired about the learning commons approach from presentations and activities sharing the literature and research, or from being mentored by other educators such as the principal or teacher-librarian, encouraging them to take part. These steering team representative teachers look forward to engaging their fellow teachers and students in moving the approach forward, and want to learn more about using innovative approaches for learning and teaching. In an article addressed to teachers, Loertscher and Koechlin (2011) write in response to reported teacher concerns regarding effective use of technology for learning and how a learning commons responds to teachers in addressing these needs. They provide ideas to consider, in how the learning commons approach supports teachers to "build a whole new way of learning" (Loertscher and Koechlin, 2011). Teachers learn how to or continue to "utilize the teacher-librarian (T-L) by bringing expertise in content to the Learning Commons, and then work with the T-L to develop engaging instructional and learning strategies" (McVittie and Duggan, 2014). Teacher representatives on the steering team provide essential teacher voice, concerns, and ideas for learning commons growth and development throughout classrooms. They also encourage fellow educators in grades, subjects, and departments to utilize and explore co-teaching, planning, and assessment through the approach. They do this informally in conversation, department meetings, and so on, or formally by actively creating and implementing professional development activities or action research projects with the steering team.

Library technicians, librarians, and other school library support staff, such as assistants or clerks working in the school library learning commons, are "critical to managing and maintaining best resource collections, facilities and technologies for modern learning. These important players support the entire learning commons community and may be on site at the school, travelling between multiple schools or working centrally to keep information systems running" (Canadian Library Association, 2014b, p. 22) Many school library learning commons support staff hold professional certification in their field, but if they do not have teacher certification they do not co-plan, design, teach, or assess curricular learning experiences. These key library professionals support teachers and teacher-librarians in their instructional roles, and under the direction of teacher-librarians and teachers, assist students in the use and operation of resources. School library learning commons support staff conduct many technical operations in the physical and virtual learning commons, freeing the teacher-librarian or learning commons lead teacher and classroom teachers to focus on collaborative planning, teaching, and assessment. This technical work includes duties such as circulation and maintenance of print and digital resources, reference question assistance, managing the library catalogue, and handling interlibrary loans. Library technicians with certification from a post-secondary institution carry out additional duties such as cataloguing learning resources, and managing and customizing online databases and networks. As part of the steering team, library support staff articulate for and sustain high standards for learning environments focused on collaboration. They engage and welcome learning community members in both the physical and virtual commons.

> Support personnel include technicians, clerical assistants and any other assistants who work in the learning commons or computer laboratory. These support persons take on the major responsibility of the "warehouse" under the direction of the teacher technologist and teacher-librarian who are concentrating the bulk of their time on improving instruction. Support personnel may have credentials, such as certificates in technology, or have had short courses in the operation of the functions of the open commons. They keep networks up and running, keep collections circulating and handle the calendars of the open commons and the computer lab for scheduled classes and free flow of individuals, small groups and full classes that do not require the services of the professionals. Besides training, these personnel are very organized, friendly, service oriented, and problem solvers. They understand and are able to implement client-side policies established by the professionals in order to make the learning commons attractive to both students and teachers alike. (Loertscher, Koechlin, and Zwaan, 2008, p. 72)

Other support staff members such as educational assistants may also support teachers and teacher-librarians in their instructional roles and, under the direction of teacher-librarians and teachers, assist students in learning in the classroom and throughout the school, including learning commons experiences and spaces. Some educational assistants work with a fixed group of students or a single student; others support students on an interchangeable schedule. Other support staff members in a school may occasionally volunteer to be members of the steering team, and bring knowledge of supporting a range of diverse student needs.

Students enjoy, learn from, and bring or generate many ideas when involved on steering teams. Their involvement varies with the context, size, and grade configuration of a school. For example, an elementary school has two sixth graders as student representatives on a learning commons steering team. The representative students then provide the team with ideas for developing the learning commons by surveying other students, accomplished in a variety of ways. Other students rotate representation, to offer a chance for greater student participation. Another way to involve more students in either elementary or secondary schools is to have each classroom or grade select or elect (in a democratic school model) two volunteer student representatives for a learning commons student leadership club that the teacher-librarian or learning commons lead teacher organizes. Student learning commons representation within student leadership structures, such as student councils, provide representatives who could gather ideas from the student body about transforming the school library into a learning commons approach. Student representatives learn about engaging, gathering, synthesizing, analyzing, and putting into motion fellow students' ideas for the approach, using various types of surveys or focus groups both in real time and through social media. Students learn how to engage fellow students to ensure that the school library to learning commons transformation reflects a wide variety of student needs and interests. In Toronto, Ontario, a school librarian specialist, consultant, and architectural coordinator developed a website for designing school library learning commons spaces for teens, including strategies for how to engage teens in the process through using technology, as "technology is seamlessly interwoven into all aspects of their lives, for communicating, socializing, researching, collaborating for learning, playing and creating" (Brooks Kirkland, Koechlin, and Di Sabatino, 2013).

Students also engage the community through extending learning commons projects and experiences to help others in local and far-reaching global communities. Steering team students form, lead, and implement ideas focusing on citizenship and philanthropy. Subjects such as environmental studies are found throughout the grades and curriculum, with students involved in research projects relating to the environment—ecosystems, endangered species, fossil fuels, and many other topics and issues of study. Extending a study of environmental awareness in science, student groups of all ages participate in improving their own school grounds with natural or vegetable gardens, studying which species grow best in their climate and engaging other students, teachers, parents, neighbors near the school, the school district garden department, and so on, to create and take care of natural spaces that they use for multiple purposes—study, research, reading, painting, or food preparation with a vegetable garden. Extending further into the community and partnering with the local food bank, students ensure food that they grow is donated to the organization. Opportunities for student engagement with the community nearby or far away are developed from many co-taught learning commons projects—from students becoming technology mentors within the school (Ramsey, 2010), to students providing a secondary school in Kenya with an irrigation system to vastly improve water sourcing for growing food (Knittel, 2012).

Parent representation on the steering committee comes about in a variety of ways, again dependent on the context of the school and how parent involvement in the school occurs. In some schools the principal requests that the school needs a formal parent representative for the learning commons steering team, to be selected or volunteer from the parent-teacher association (PTA). The parent from the PTA provides input to the steering team, as well as reports back to the PTA regarding the concept of the school library to learning commons approach, its benefits to student learning, its progress, and how the PTA can contribute ideas and support. In other schools a dedicated school library parent volunteer joins the team to act as the liaison between the school, the PTA, and the broader community. Parent representatives help communicate learning commons transformation goals and activities to the parent community, engage other parents in the development, and celebrate the impact that the approach has on student learning. Once parents see and understand this impact, their support for the growth and sustainability of the approach grows in many valuable ways. When school libraries in Spokane, WA, were facing budget cuts to their teacher-librarians in 2008, three parents who highly valued the impact of the school library on their children's learning worked tirelessly with the state to re-secure funding and succeeded in their aim to "save their school libraries" and teacher-librarians. In doing so, they created a model for other parents to follow. Two key motivations that kept them fighting for their school libraries were, first of all, that their children had had firsthand experience with effective teacher-librarians; and secondly, they had learned about the school library impact studies (Library Research Service, 2013) that demonstrated through educational research the impact of school libraries and teacher-librarians on student achievement (Murvosh, 2013; Whelan, 2008).

The American Association of School Librarians (AASL) provides extensive information through a "Parent Advocate Toolkit" on the AASL website, designed for parents to build their understanding of the role school libraries play in impacting their child's learning, which the learning commons approach takes forward. This includes information on how parents can get involved and advocate for their school library, the AASL *Standards for the 21st-Century Learner* (American Association of School Librarians, 2007), what to look for in an effective school library, what the school library student learning impact studies say, and much more (American Association of School Librarians, 2016e). Steering teams can use and link to such information to engage and inform parents. PTAs often help raise welcome funds for school library to learning commons enhancement; additionally, parent representation builds learning commons volunteers to lend a hand in many ways. Parents become engaged in the learning commons approach by volunteering their expertise to collaborative projects and learning experiences, such as a parent who is a geologist taking part in a science project, or parent who is a historian taking part in a social studies project.

The WSLLC steering team is aware of and promotes civic, state, provincial, or territorial library services and provisions that enhance the learning commons services and approach. The steering team engages associates or members from the nearest branch of the public library. Librarians from the public library can visit schools K–12 to inform students about their programs and services; or classes might visit the public library to learn about them. In many public libraries, this is part of the librarian's outreach role. A librarian from the local public library branch might be interested in becoming a member of the steering team, with interest to plan for contextually appropriate ways that the public library and school library learning commons collaborate. The public library branch itself might use or explore a learning commons approach.

Many states, provinces, and territories offer online library resources and services, through the library or education ministries having licensing arrangements that provide schools with reference resources, e-books, and databases for free or minimal expense, subsidized by government monies or grants. Each type of library—school, public, or academic—serves as a gateway to quality resources and collaborative tools. Knowing how to access and use these services is fiscally wise in less purchasing of reference works, data bases, or e-book collections; as well as wise in facilitating students' and staff's ability to use the resources to support thinking and learning. For instance, to date, the Texas State Library and Archives Commission provides K–12 services such as TexQuest, "which provides up-to-date, authoritative, non-commercial educational resources for every grade level and subject area" (Texas State Library and Archives Commission, 2016b), as well as other school library services such as the "Talking Book Program"—"a free service that loans books and magazines to people who cannot read standard print publications because of visual, physical, or reading disabilities" (Texas State Library and Archives Commission, 2016a). In Alberta, Canada, through the Alberta Library Consortium, students are provided with online licensed resources, and teachers with professional development in their use, through an online reference center subsidized with a "Grant-in-Aid" from the government (The Alberta Library, 2016). Collaborative work between community library sectors in many states and provinces promotes systems in place for seamless access to resources and services that can engage the community throughout their lives, including specialized services for inclusive educational needs.

In some communities, particularly smaller ones, the public library is housed in the school, using a variety of configurations and agreements, and is a focal point for the community: "Connect[ing] with a larger network, regional system, or consortia…no library can operate on its own any longer…. Collaborative efforts enable us to leverage our resources for greater effect and see possibilities that may include co-location after full exploration of all of the alternatives and options" (Haycock, 2006). Again, one of the factors of success of school-housed public libraries for students that Haycock points out is that "the principal of the school should have a strong desire for success and teachers should support the concept," and that the most successful combinations occur when "equal partners solve common community problems together and the level of service must be at least equal to, or better than, two separate entities." Schools with school-housed public libraries can develop a learning commons approach through forming a steering team, where the librarian working for the public library in the school-housed library is a member or leader of the team, as the school may not have a teacher-librarian. The public librarian works with the school in developing ways to support learning and extend into the community—for instance, in the example of co-creating a joint family literacy initiative to meet outcomes shared by both the school and the public library. This type of cooperation, collaboration, and talent required of principals, teachers, and public librarians in schools housing the public library, works toward engaging the learning community and its resident library in a learning commons approach.

When engaging any facet of the community, proponents will likely come across the view that school libraries or libraries in general face obsolescence. A key point in counteracting that view is reinforcing the importance of heightening the engagement of youth, from kindergarten through grade 12, with information and learning in community spaces and places, and inviting members of the broader community into schools through live or virtual events such as author readings or "bringing in a local celebrity to discuss a book or media trend" (Lynch, 2015). Engaging students with authors and experts from the local or broader community can be arranged in many ways, from writing or e-mailing student responses to literature or questions for experts, to fully funded author or expert residencies. The school library learning commons is often the first or only experience students have engaging with authors, where they learn more about the creative process involved in bringing what they read to another dimension and have the joy of reading promoted. Authors and experts who live near the school in the local community provide expanded knowledge of local publications and are easier to arrange visits, workshops, or partnerships with, such as serving as a school's own "author [or expert] in residence." Residencies involving authors, teacher-librarians, and classroom teachers benefit reading or English studies—and can also engage and benefit across the curriculum, when schools involve science writers, art writers, and others across subject areas and disciplines. Authors from the local community or beyond, including popular authors, are often available for presentations, could be on tour nearby, or might even be open to partnering online. Most publisher sites have information about author visits and contacting authors, and most authors have their own websites with contact information. Experts in many subject areas can be contacted through topic-specific sites such as well-known science or other organizations. Schools may also discover authors or experts within their parent community. Authors and experts provide a supportive community voice and occasionally become members of steering teams, depending on how involved they become with the school.

Many school districts engage their schools in transforming their school libraries through collaborative district initiatives. These districts bring together principals, teacher-librarians, and other steering team members for professional learning related to school libraries and learning commons, so that achieving district goals and outcomes becomes a dedicated part of the school library to learning commons approach. School district library learning commons specialists occasionally become members of a steering team or teams, to provide the teams with on-site leadership, support, and direction. They help facilitate learning commons approach articulation between schools or across multiple school sites, so that student learning is supported equitably throughout the district with similar approaches, standards, expectations, resources, and technology, including resources that are provided by and available from the district. Often the school library learning commons district specialist is a teacher-librarian who brings their background knowledge and leadership to the district and provides current information on district, state, provincial, or territorial pedagogical news and events in rapidly changing areas such as learning commons and technology for learning.

WSLLC development involves all educators in the school and the steering team in strategically engaging the community:

> To ensure that the physical library learning commons is maximized to its potential it needs to be open and ready for learning at all times. Students and teachers need to know that real time support, expertise, resources and technologies are always available and that the LLC is a stable extension of every classroom. The virtual learning commons provides a 24/7 environment for teachers and students to work, create and share anytime. Together the two learning environments provide diverse opportunities to naturally bridge the gap between isolated classrooms and the networked worlds of modern learning. (Canadian Library Association, 2014b, p. 36)

Schools differ in context, yet every school has a principal who can initiate the approach. Many schools have teacher-librarians, other administrators, technology teachers, or learning commons teachers collaborating to provide learners with collaborative learning experiences, instructional guidance, and access to resources. Some schools do not have learning commons educational specialists or expertise. They may be very small schools, schools impacted by budgetary decisions, or schools unfamiliar with learning commons pedagogy and its demonstrated effect on improving student learning. In these cases the principal, steering team, and members of the learning community must explore creative solutions to garnering learning commons expertise within their school and district. *Leading Learning: Standards of Practice for School Library Learning Commons in Canada* presents a list of scenarios for schools to consider and add to (Canadian Library Association, 2014b, p. 36).

The process of engaging the community can be summarized through the following reminders. Start exploring the learning commons approach together as a faculty, and invest time and effort into activities such as those suggested in this book, for developing a shared vision your school library to learning commons transformation. Infuse learning commons plans into the school development plan and instructional programs. Form a steering team to lead the vision and action planning, and include the leadership of a teacher-librarian or learning commons lead teacher. Employ a variety of mentorship techniques within and beyond the team, to bring everyone along. Collaboratively collect and analyze student learning data, to inform and develop the learning commons design, plans, and actions, based on curricular learning outcomes and the co-determined inclusive needs of all students. Set pedagogical and budget goals for rich physical and virtual learning environments in stages, based on the learning needs of each student, working toward optimal resource levels for collections and staffing. Collaboratively plan, teach, and assess learning experiences and events with active student participation, to attain the curricular mandate outcomes. Know, align with, keep current on, share, and discuss learning commons approach literature, research, policies, and standards. Share the learning commons plan with the learning community, and engage the community in its experiences, news, and developments on an ongoing basis. Demonstrate accountability through cyclic site-based research processes—gather, analyze, and share evidence of student learning impact. Provide time for deep learning, thinking, and making, as well as time for professional learning opportunities along the way and into the future. Celebrate successes and keep on growing. And don't forget to connect with others who are on the WSLLC journey! Mentor, and be accountable for learning, knowing, and contributing to learning commons literature and research, and engaging the learning community.

Three Keys to Unlock WSLLC:

- Active leadership of the principal
- Co-teaching and collaboration
- Base on student need from student data

Chapter 9

SELECTED RESOURCES WITH STRATEGIES FOR COMMUNITY ENGAGEMENT

Although the learning commons will look and feel different in every school, it must be the center of inquiry, digital citizenship, project-based learning, collaborative intelligence, advanced literacy as well as the center of creating, performing, and sharing. It will sometimes take on a role as "third space," neither home nor school. It is the place young people love—their space. (Loertscher and Koechlin, 2014, p. E4)

Strategies for creating shared ownership of the WSLLC are multifaceted. Some schools engage all of the community at once; others engage primarily teachers or students, especially in the early stages of development. Often the suggested strategies or resources intersect with each other, so you can use them at many entry points in engaging the community to develop and sustain exemplary learning commons spaces and approaches. Use or adapt the strategies that follow, and add additional resources from the selected ones as contextually pertinent.

WSLLC Community Resource 1:

"Did You Know? Shift Happens, 2014 Remix" (Fisch, McLeod, and Brenman, 2014)

WSLLC Community Strategy 1:

Introducing Change

The video slideshow suggested for this activity, "Did You Know? Shift Happens, 2014 Remix" (Fisch, McLeod, and Brenman, 2014), is a remix of a five-minute presentation showcasing rapid technological and demographic change in the world, set to a lively musical background. Use it to start conversation about change in moving from a school library to a learning commons approach. Through numbers and quotations, the remix illustrates the exponential increase of technology and change in society, with a wide variety of interesting statements delivered in a comparative format to show how rapidly change is occurring in the last few years of human history compared to the past—and how much more things will rapidly change in the future, looking at dramatic developments in areas of technology, human knowledge, careers, and more. Statements such as "90% of the world's data has been generated in the past two years" lead to a conclusion with the significant question: "But what does it all mean?" After viewing the video at a staff meeting, during a professional day, in a steering team meeting, in class with students, or at a PTA meeting, have the principal, teacher-librarian, or other facilitator lead a discussion using this question and creating other guiding questions based on context. Give participants time to brainstorm responses to questions as individuals or in small groups, and share and summarize responses. Try these questions:

1. "What does it all mean?"
2. What do you think is rapidly changing in school libraries today?
3. How do you think school libraries will look in the future?
4. "What does it all mean" for transitioning the school library into a learning commons approach? Why change?
5. Have we changed enough, or how do we lead into the future?

Once participants have time to think about, discuss, and process the questions through writing or drawing, have groups such as students and steering teams create their own brief remix with music, to illustrate why and how school libraries are changing to the learning commons approach, and how to develop that in the context of their school. Post and share the presentations on the virtual learning commons to engage the broader community.

WSLLC Community Resource 2:

"The School Tech Squad: A Learning Commons Technology Boost" (Ramsey, 2010)

WSLLC Community Strategy 2:

Finding More Time to Engage Community in WSLLC

Finding enough time to do everything is one of the biggest stressors in life or work today, and life/work balance is critical to health and well-being. Educators' work is multifaceted and multidimensional, and faculties usually do many things at once in highly busy environments such as a school library. What are some ways educators address the issue of time with implementing a learning commons approach, engaging the immediate faculty and students and the broader community? Use the foundation of learning commons pedagogy—co-planning and teaching around co-determined student learning needs; both parties save time and build practice. Schedule common collaborative planning time and flexible learning commons timetables. Mentor on-site and in real or online networks, to provide ideas and gain experience by learning from others. Harness the power of students in generative ways, such as student tech squads, to not only save time but also provide students with authentic social learning opportunities and involvement in the learning commons development. The article "The School Tech Squad: A Learning Commons Technology Boost" (Ramsey, 2010) describes the power of a student group who transformed their school, teachers, library to learning commons, and selves through becoming technology mentors to teachers across a high school.

The pressures of time say a lot about our culture and the culture of the education profession and schools. It is inevitable to yearn for more time, with so many things to accomplish every day while educating students for success in the broader, busy culture. Stop to consider how the time rush affects educators and students in their learning. Do students have sufficient time to engage in deep learning through co-taught learning experiences? Do students have time before, during, and after the instructional day, along with support in the physical or virtual commons for studies and projects? We yearn for more hours in a day, yet when we take the time to reflect on where time is spent, it can be illuminating—and "extra" hours for deep learning and engaging the broader community can be found. Use a time log, such as the chart below, to keep track of your time as a self-reflective activity for an average school week, or as a steering team or faculty activity with follow-up discussion. Complete the time chart, and brainstorm possibilities for finding time for the key components of learning commons development to impact student learning. Use these questions to consider and discuss the time chart:

- What impressions do you have of your use of time over the week?
- How does your use of time inform your learning commons collaborative work with faculty, students, and the broader community?
- Which activities did you engage in that you think had the most positive impact in your role for students? Why?
- What other observations or reflections do you have about your time?

Sample Time Chart

Week Day	Time Spent Co-planning/ Assessing Collaborative WSLLC Learning Experiences	Time Spent Co-Teaching WSLLC Learning Experiences	Time with Individual Students or Faculty	Time with Parents/ Community Members	Time Spent Other Ways

> **WSLLC Community Resource 3:**
> *Leading Learning: Standards of Practice for School Library Learning Commons in Canada* (Canadian Library Association, 2014b, pp. 21, 23, 27)
>
> **WSLLC Community Strategy 3:**
> Changing Roles Reflections

The WSLLC development is best guided and facilitated through steering teams, rooted in the philosophy and practice of "collaborative professional learning teams in professional learning communities" (DuFour, DuFour, Eaker, and Karhnek, 2004). What these teams look like, their members, how they form, and what the team needs to know and understand at any given site varies based on individual school needs and context. Generally, the core steering team includes the principal and/or other school administrators, a teacher-librarian or lead learning commons teacher, other subject teacher(s), and library support personnel. The glossary of *Leading Learning: Standards of Practice for School Library Learning Commons in Canada* (Canadian Library Association, 2014b, p. 27) provides summaries of roles and responsibilities related to the school library learning commons that will be familiar to some members and new to others.

Use table 9.1 with your steering team to reflect and discuss changing roles and responsibilities relating to the learning commons approach, as summarized in the table. Have the team discuss what to add regarding their role, what they find challenging in their role changing, and what areas they need more information or professional development in. Develop an action plan as a team to address the challenges and professional development needs. Share reflections and plans with the faculty, inviting them into a broader conversation about changing roles and responsibilities in the learning commons approach.

Table 9.1 WSLLC Steering Team Role Reflections

ROLE SUMMARY*	Additions to Current WSLLC Role	Challenges or Changes to WSLLC Role	Information/ Professional Development Needs for Current WSLLC Role
Principal: *Curriculum leaders and school site managers; provide leadership, budgets, and support for moving forward with library learning commons (LLC)*			
Teacher-Librarian: *Teacher who leads the LLC program and has education in school librarianship*			
Teacher-Technologist: *Co-teacher in the LLC model's effective and transformative uses of technology; has education in technology*			
Learning Commons Teacher: *Teacher assigned responsibilities for management/program in the LLC when there is no teacher-librarian*			
Teacher: *Establish instructional designs that engage learners in developing 21st-century skills, literacies, and knowledge-building, through utilization of exemplary technologies and resources*			
Library Technician: *Assists LLC team with LLC management; has library/information technology diploma*			

*Summarized from *Leading Learning: Standards of Practice for School Library Learning Commons in Canada* (Canadian Library Association, 2014b, pp. 21, 23, 27).

WSLLC Community Resource 4:
"Technology and the Learning Commons" (Marcoux, 2015)

WSLLC Community Strategy 4:
Defining Our WSLLC

In the growing literature and research relating to school library learning commons, learning commons pioneers, experts, and practitioners provide a variety of analogous definitions or descriptions of the school library learning commons. This book references descriptions from the book *The Virtual Learning Commons* (Loertscher, Koechlin, and Rosenfeld, 2012), and from *Leading Learning* (Canadian Library Association, 2014b, p. 5). In the article "Technology and the Learning Commons" (Marcoux, 2015), a description of the learning commons focuses on the relation of the approach to technology in learning:

> The Learning Commons is an extension of what most of us have known as the school library. The differences between them are subtle but big. The school library is about control, the Learning Commons is about on-demand. The school library is organization based; the Learning Commons is client based. Technology in a school library is used to augment what information is available; technology in the Learning Commons is used to create and consume information in addition to finding it, regardless of its locale. The Learning Commons is a laboratory that is used by all learners—faculty and students alike—to develop their information while improving their skills with technology. Creative experimentation is encouraged at all levels. Professional development is something that all ages can participate in. The Learning Commons is a place where networks, applications, and access are technologically supported to facilitate ideas that lead to learning. A collaborative atmosphere between teachers, students, and caregivers exists to improve each and everyone's abilities to use whatever technology is needed to advance learning. (Marcoux, 2015, p. 65)

Have your steering team (or principal or teacher-librarian, if a steering team is not yet in place) share these and other definitions and descriptions of the school library learning commons at a staff meeting or on a professional day. Organize participants into groups, and request that the groups study the learning commons definitions in relation to their own school library to learning commons context. Ask them to respond to the definitions/descriptions in light of their own context, using the letters "WSLLC" to compose an acrostic poem comprising a sentence or two to describe their vision or observations for the school's approach. Share, collect, amalgamate, and post; the acrostics give the principal and steering team insight into preparing a school definition or description of learning commons and ideas for next steps.

You can also engage students in this activity of writing acrostic poems with their ideas for the learning commons. Organize a classroom door decorating "learning commons design contest." Have the teacher-librarian, steering team student leaders, and teachers speak to classes about the school library changing and developing into a learning commons approach, and invite student ideas through the contest. Ask the students to envision their school library's future. Cover classroom doors with craft or poster paper and the large letters "WSLLC" in a vertical row on the doors. Have students write, draw, paint, or collage over a period of time what their ideas, wishes, or designs are for the school learning commons. Decide whether you will "reward" all classrooms or have a student committee select a few prominent examples of "decorating," while emphasizing that all ideas presented have value for consideration. Incorporate student ideas into learning commons planning, and post photos of designed doors on the virtual commons.

WSLLC Community Resource 5:

"Makerspaces in the School Library Learning Commons and the uTEC Maker Model" (Loertscher, Preddy, and Derry, 2013)

WSLLC Community Strategy 5:

Engaging Students through Making

"Makerspaces" in the learning commons provide a forum for student engagement. Educators familiar with makerspaces pedagogy facilitate its use through collaboratively planned and taught learning experiences. In the article "Makerspaces in the School Library Learning Commons and the uTEC Maker Model" (Loertscher, Preddy, and Derry, 2013), the authors define the growing movement of makerspaces in schools and school library learning commons, and include a maker model, uTEC, recommend resources for makerspaces, and provide examples from schools incorporating makerspaces into learning and teaching in the learning commons.

Study the uTEC model at a staff meeting, professional day, steering team meeting, or co-teaching planning session by reading the article. Read in jigsaw style, assigning article sections to individuals or groups (depending on the size of the faculty or team), and have them read and summarize the content under each heading from the article assigned to them. Brainstorm applications from the article to use in the learning commons makerspace technique, and list questions or comments that occur to participants as they read their selection or hear the others report.

Give article readers a printed or digital copy of the uTEC model to view. Once they have read, summarized, and discussed the article, they have a copy of the model to refer to for use in classroom or learning commons applications. Use the following chart to facilitate the activity and record responses; also use the chart when employing the jigsaw technique with other articles. Collect responses to inform learning commons planning.

Article: *Makerspaces in the School Library Learning Commons and the uTEC Maker Model* (Loertscher, Preddy, and Derry, 2013)	Article Section to Review	Section Summary	Applications for own WSLLC	Questions, or I'd Like to Learn More About ...
Group (or Individual) 1	*What Is a Makerspace?*			
2	*What Is a Maker?*			
3	*Traditional Making in the School Library*			
4	*The uTEC Maker Model*			
5	*Formal and Informal Education*			
6	*The Development of Makerspaces in the School Library Learning Commons*			
7	*Challenges and Opportunities*			

> **WSLLC Community Resource 6:**
> "Beattie Library Upgrades 2013" (Kamloops School District No. 73, 2013)
>
> **WSLLC Community Strategy 6:**
> Infomercials

"Infomercials" are a way to connect and communicate in engaging the broader community in your learning commons developments. In the selected brief video involving students, a school library in British Columbia depicts upgrades to their physical learning commons that the students are enthusiastic about. Share the video with the faculty or steering team, to provide inspiration for making a similar production for your own learning commons developments to post on the virtual learning commons, highlighting changes students are excited about. Create a brief (one minute or so) commercial or infomercial, "advertising" what is successfully happening with learning commons development. Involve students in the making, and inform and celebrate what the school is proud of in school library to learning commons growth and development accomplishments. Have fun and collaborate. Instead of a video, you could create a slideshow, community page on the virtual learning commons, animoto, or other visual. Have a number of schools in a community or network challenge each other to create infomercials using whatever medium they choose, and share them in network meetings or online. Sharing infomercials among schools results in new ideas and perspectives on learning commons development.

WSLLC Community Resource 7:

"Concord-Carlisle Transitions to a Learning Commons" (Cicchetti, 2010) and
"Planning and Creating a Library Learning Commons" (Hyman, 2014)

WSLLC Community Strategy 7:
WSLLC in Ten Steps

This activity synthesizes key steps for engaging the community and developing the learning commons approach for steering teams, teacher-librarian networks, or faculties. Following preliminary meetings in which participants become familiar with learning commons literature, research, and developments, ask participants to draw upon their enhanced or newly found learning commons expertise to present "How to Have a WSLLC in Ten Steps" as a brief presentation to share with the community or learning commons networks when meeting in person or on the virtual learning commons. The articles mentioned in this strategy, written by two award-winning teacher-librarians, reflect on and share the school library to learning commons approach steps taken in two schools with varying contexts. These articles, or others like them, provide a "refresher" or comparison points to note prior to engaging in the activity focused on steps in your own school. Early learning commons adopter Cicchetti writes about steps taken in the transformation of a large high school in Boston, where she continues to advance the learning commons approach; Hyman reflects on opening up a new large elementary school in Virginia. Both articles take readers through "steps," challenges, and successes in developing all aspects of a learning commons approach—physical, virtual, and pedagogical, involving and engaging their learning communities. Use the following sentence stems for participants to outline the "how-to steps."

"How to" Develop a WSLLC in Ten Steps:

1. Create ...
2. Share ...
3. Explore ...
4. Examine ...

5. Learn from …

6. Visit …

7. Study …

8. Read …

9. Connect …

10. Know …

WSLLC Community Resource 8:

"Learning commons in BC" (British Columbia Ministry of Education, 2012)

WSLLC Community Strategy 8:

Circle Brainstorm

Engage educators in brainstorming their ideal school library to learning commons approach through a circle story activity. Prepare them for the activity by having principals, teacher-librarians, or steering teams share an article or short presentation to introduce or update them on the learning commons concept. The video suggested for this strategy depicts a wide range of stages in the learning commons approach, from kindergarten through university, creating an overall view. Once participants have viewed the video, arrange chairs into a circle. Begin the circle brainstorm by giving the lead sentence: "One thing I would like to see in our WSLLC is…" The idea is then developed by the group, who add one sentence or so at a time, going around the circle. Go around the circle a number of times, to give everyone a chance to respond and contribute, as some participants will initially "pass" when it comes to their turn to speak. Gather the ideas to use in future planning.

WSLLC Community Resource 9:

"Pedagogical Shifts Inherent in the Learning Commons" ("Together for Learning," Ontario Library Association, 2016)

WSLLC Community Strategy 9:

How Does the WSLLC Pedagogical Shift Look in My Practice?

Learning commons pedagogical shifts are succinctly summarized in figure 9.1, "Pedagogical Shifts Inherent in the Learning Commons," which we introduced in the preface of this book.

Information Seeking and Reporting		Individual and Collective Knowledge Creation
Teacher-directed learning	→	Self and participatory learning
Classroom learning	→	Networked and global learning
Standards-driven	→	Exploring big ideas and concepts
Teaching	→	Process and active learning
Individual teacher expertise	→	Collaborative learning partnerships

Figure 9.1 Pedagogical Shifts Inherent in the Learning Commons (Ontario School Library Association, 2010, p. 35)

Have the principal, teacher-librarian, or steering team lead educators to reflect individually on these five pedagogical shifts, and record their thoughts using the following chart. Ask for volunteers to share some of their reflections and ideas to discuss in small groups, and to keep these in mind as they initiate instructional planning—particularly when co-planning with a teacher-librarian, or lead learning commons teacher, and other classroom or subject teachers. Encourage educators who provide examples of making the pedagogical shift in their practice to share the examples on the virtual learning commons, to celebrate with the learning community.

WSLLC Pedagogical Shift

Examples in my practice where I have made this pedagogical shift	Ideas to make this pedagogical shift in my practice	Ideas to make this pedagogical shift in a WSLLC co-teaching experience
Self and Participatory Learning:		
Networked and Global Learning:		
Exploring Big Ideas and Concepts:		
Process and Active Learning:		
Collaborative Learning Partnerships:		

Source: OLA, 2016

WSLLC Community Resource 10:
St. Joseph High School Hosts Human Library (Todd, 2015)

WSLLC Community Strategy 10:
"Human Libraries"

The concept of "human libraries," or community members who act as "living books" to speak with small groups of students, represent a variety of careers, backgrounds, and interests to engage students and community members as part of the learning commons approach. Many public libraries embrace the concept, with schools starting to develop it:

> Human Library events were first developed in Europe to allow readers to meet with people from diverse backgrounds in an effort to break down stereotypes and prejudices. These events have been successful in bringing community members together, fostering diversity and changing attitudes. In a 21st Century Learning environment, Human Library events also reinforce the role of a library as a Learning Commons, an important place to bring diverse people together, to provide meaningful social action among students and community members. Students will be given the opportunity to hear diverse stories and converse with a wide variety of community members. Human Library volunteers are essentially living books that can be borrowed by KLO readers for a set period of time (15–20 minutes) to engage in conversations. (Central Okanagan School District, 2015)

A number of schools in the Central Okanagan district participate in engaging the community through the learning commons by holding human library events. A middle school in the same district mentions the wide range of community members volunteering to participate in the events:

> Examples of "books" might be extreme athletes, songwriters, authors, rock musicians, people with physical challenges, people with survival stories (disease or event), musicians, new immigrants, police officers, parole officers, teen mothers, refugees, city officials, veterans, activists, actors, models, body builders, vegans, funeral directors, exaddicts, retirees, SPCA representatives, social media experts etc. Students will reserve their Human Book ahead of time and come prepared with questions, but volunteering community members are asked to come with a prepared 5–10 minute presentation. The atmosphere is informal, with 2–8 students signing out a "book" at a time. (Central Okanagan School District, 2013.)

News reports posted on a Vancouver, British Columbia, secondary school learning commons blog also reflect the range of community members taking part (Gladstone Library Learning Commons, 2012).

Introduce educators to the human library concept through viewing the short one-minute news video clip in this strategy, an example of how a senior high school in Ottawa highlights a human library event. The teacher-librarian and other educators in the clip collaboratively planned a cross-curricular "Digital Citizenship Human Library" to "allow students to interact people who work with social media on a daily basis" (Todd, 2015). Share additional information on human libraries from other sources mentioned here or known to you. After introducing the human library concept, discuss ideas to implement it in your learning commons, using the following questions:

- How does the human library concept connect with curricular learning, student learning needs, and the school development plan goals?
- Does it focus on a cross-curricular topic such as social media, or do we invite a wide variety of presenters from the community and connect the expertise that is volunteered with curricular events?
- How does the human library complement or extend current or future learning commons co-planned and taught experiences? (Community is often a topic in primary school curriculum.)
- Does the living books concept become a special event focused on learning more about the community and its members?
- What details do we attend to in the organization of a human library? Who is responsible and for what?
- How is the human library experience shared? On what platforms?

Following agreement on these questions and others that are contextually relevant, send letters introducing the human library concept to the community, to invite participation.

WSLLC Community Resource 11:
Guiding Principles for the Learning Commons Grant Program (Domeier de Suarez, 2012)

WSLLC Community Strategy 11:
Write a WSLLC Proposal

Engage the community in collaboratively writing a proposal for enhanced support for the WSLLC, and involve immediate and adjacent learning community members. Write the proposal to the school district as part of a school improvement plan goal; some districts invite proposals either specifically for library to learning commons, or for technology or instructional improvements or innovation. Schools also direct proposals to granting agencies, and in the United States there are quite a few of these related to school library enhancement. In any type of proposal requesting support for enhancement or innovation, directly show how the innovation—in this case the WSLLC—inclusively impacts student learning. Many books and websites have been developed for finding and attaining educational grants and grants for school libraries, such as those listed on the "Grant Resources" page on the blog "Renovated Learning" (Rendina, 2015). Most granting agencies post tips for attaining a grant from them, and some include examples of successful grant applications (Indigo Love of Reading Foundation, 2016).

Proposals or grants directly pertaining to enhancing learning commons are rare but increasing, as schools applying for school library enhancement grants or district proposals do so in the spirit of shifting from school library to the learning commons approach. "Guiding Principles for a Learning Commons Grant Program"—compiled by district level teacher-librarian Domeier de Suarez for applying to a district grant in Surrey, British Columbia, to fund innovative learning design projects—shows an example of an application focused on a learning commons approach. This district offers funding targeted mostly to technology hardware and furnishings, and includes a staff development component, both of which the writer found applicable to learning commons development. The guidelines in this proposal example point out key learning commons approach factors to keep in mind for proposals, including "ensuring that the project clearly and specifically articulates how student engagement and student learning will be enhanced and how all the members of the school community will be invested in the Learning Commons experience" (Domeier de Suarez, 2012, p. 6).

Have the principal, teacher-librarian, and steering team study these guidelines or others like them along with the literature and research focused on learning commons. Prepare an initial draft for a district or granting agency proposal to assist with learning commons development. Important information for such a proposal includes:

- Start the proposal with program: collaborative planning, teaching, and assessing focused on specific student learning goals and outcomes;
- Link the program components to school, district, and provincial or territorial initiatives and goals;
- Outline how a modified physical learning commons environment will support student learning program and goals;
- Outline how a modified virtual learning commons environment will enhance the physical spaces and work in tandem to support student learning programs and goals;
- Have steering team members provide statements from their perspective on how the learning commons enhancement impacts student learning.

Share a draft of the proposal with the faculty, students groups, and PTA as pertinent, to gain further insight, feedback, and input or questions regarding the proposal. Once most community members agree on the proposal, submit it to the district or granting agency. With the whole school community behind the WSLLC proposal, it is sure to be successfully attained.

BIBLIOGRAPHY

Abilock, D., V. Harada, and K. Fontichiaro, eds. 2012. *Growing Schools: Librarians as Professional Developers.* Santa Barbara, CA: ABC-CLIO.

Achterman, Doug. 2007. "The Sower: Interview with Keith Curry Lance." *School Library Journal* 53 (10): 50–53. Available: http://www.slj.com/2007/10/interviews/the-sower -interview-with-keith-curry-lance/#_ (accessed January 1, 2016).

Alberta Education. 2016. "Learning Commons/School Libraries." Available: https:// education.alberta.ca/learning-commons/learning-commons/ (accessed April 27, 2016).

Alberta's Education Partners. 2010, Rev. July 2012. "A Guide to Support Implementation: Essential Conditions." Available: http://www.essentialconditions.ca/ (accessed January 1, 2016).

Alberta Municipal Affairs. 2013. Collaborative Library Policy. Available: http://www .municipalaffairs.alberta.ca/documents/lcvss/Government_of_Alberta-Collaborative _Library_Policy.pdf (accessed January 1, 2016).

Alberta School Learning Commons Council. 2015. "Library Learning Commons: What Might That Look Like?" [Video File]. Available: https://www.youtube.com/watch?v= 6wVA8EeDf_0&feature=youtu.be (accessed January 1, 2016).

Alberta Teacher's Association. 2016. Professional Growth Plans. Available: http:// www.teachers.ab.ca/For%20Members/Professional%20Development/Teacher%20 Professional%20Growth/Pages/Teacher%20Professional%20Growth%20Plans.aspx (accessed January 1, 2016).

American Association of School Librarians (AASL). 2007. *Standards for the 21st-Century Learner.* Available: http://www.ala.org/aasl/standards-guidelines/learning-standards (accessed January 1, 2016).

American Association of School Librarians (AASL). 2016a. Conferences and Meetings. Available: http://www.ala.org/aasl/conferences (accessed April 28, 2016).

American Association of School Librarians (AASL). 2016b. "Learning About the Job: Mentoring or Job Shadowing Programs." Available: http://www.ala.org/aasl/education /recruitment/learning (accessed January 1, 2016).

American Association of School Librarians (AASL). 2016c. "Learning Standards and Common Core State Standards Crosswalk." Available: http://www.ala.org/aasl/standards-guidelines/crosswalk (accessed January 1, 2016).

American Association of School Librarians (AASL). 2016d. "Library Education and Licensing." Available: http://www.ala.org/aasl/education/recruitment/licensing (accessed January 1, 2016).

American Association of School Librarians (AASL). 2016e. "Parent Advocate Toolkit." Available: http://www.ala.org/aasl/advocacy/tools/toolkits/parent-advocate (accessed May 1, 2016).

American Association of School Librarians (AASL). 2013. "Implementing the Common Core State Standards: The Role of the School Librarian." Available: http://www.ala.org/aasl/sites/ala.org.aasl/files/content/externalrelations/CCSSLibrariansBrief_FINAL.pdf (accessed January 1, 2016).

American Library Association (ALA). 2016. Carroll Preston Baber Research Grant. Available: http://www.ala.org/offices/ors/orsawards/baberresearchgrant/babercarroll (accessed January 1, 2016).

Andrea, Kevin. 2015. "Welcome to the 2015–2016 School Year!" Northern Gateway Public Schools. Available: http://www.ngps.ca/about-us/news/post/welcome-back-from-the-superintendent#.V2g7DldqdB8 (accessed June 21, 2016).

Asselin, Marlene, Jennifer L. Branch, and Dianne Oberg, eds. 2003. *Achieving Information Literacy: Standards for School Library Programs in Canada*. Ottawa, ON: Canadian School Library Association/Association for Teacher-Librarianship in Canada. Available: http://www.clatoolbox.ca/casl/slic/ (accessed January 1, 2016).

Association for Teacher-Librarianship in Canada, and Canadian School Library Association. 1997. "Students' Information Literacy Needs in the 21st Century: Competencies for Teacher-Librarians."

British Columbia Ministry of Education. 2012. "Learning Commons in BC" [Video file]. Available: http://commons.bclibraries.ca/case_study/adapting-to-21st-century-learning-the-learning-commons/ (accessed January 1, 2016).

Brooks Kirkland, Anita. 2013. "Transforming Library Spaces." *School Libraries in Canada* 31 (3). Available: http://clatoolbox.ca/casl/slicv31n3/313brookskirkland.html (accessed January 1, 2016).

Brooks Kirkland, Anita. 2015, July 1. "Leading Learning Goes International" [Web log post]. Available: http://www.bythebrooks.ca/leading-learning-goes-international/ (accessed January 1, 2016).

Brooks Kirkland, Anita. 2015, October 13. "Think You're not a Researcher? Think Again!" [Web log post]. Available: http://tmcanada.blogspot.ca/2015_10_01_archive.html (accessed January 1, 2016).

Brooks Kirkland, Anita. 2016. "By the Brooks"—Libraries and Learning: Leadership for the School Library Learning Commons. Available: http://www.bythebrooks.ca/ (accessed January 5, 2016).

Brooks Kirkland, Anita, and Carol Koechlin. 2014. "Collaborative Leadership: A Learning Commons Model." *The Trillium* 2, 5–7. Available: http://ascd.ca/ascd/on/wp-content/uploads/2011/03/Trillium-Newsletter_WEB-July-2014.pdf (accessed January 1, 2016).

Brooks Kirkland, Anita, and Carol Koechlin. 2015. "Leading Learning: Standards of Practice for School Libraries in Canada—A Catalyst for Igniting Change." *Teacher Librarian: The Journal for School Library Professionals* 42 (5): 45–47.

Brooks Kirkland, Anita, Carol Koechlin, and Sofia Di Sabatino. 2013, July 9. Teen Territories: Creating Their Special Spaces in Libraries. Available: https://sites.google.com/site/teenterritories/home (accessed January 1, 2016).

Brown, Carol A., Lana Kaye Dotson, and Elaine Yontz. 2011. "Professional Development for School Library Media Professionals." *TechTrends: Linking Research and Practice to Improve Learning* 55 (4): 56–62.

Brown, Gerald R., and Judith A. Sykes. 2016. "Assessing Effective School Library Learning Commons Themes: What Do They Look Like? What Questions Can Help Us Assess Where We Are?" Available: https://sites.google.com/site/treasuremountaincanada4 /-building-a-learning-community/sykes-and-brown (accessed April 27, 2016)

Buckley, Jeanne, and Eileen Arruda. 2014, January 31. "Mentorship of New Teacher-Librarians" [Slideshare]. Available: http://www.accessola2.com/superconference2014 /sessions/1326.pdf (accessed January 1, 2016).

California Department of Education. 2010. School Library Standards. Available: http:// www.cde.ca.gov/ci/cr/lb/schlibrarystds.asp (accessed January 1, 2016).

Cannon Design. The Third Teacher+. 2016. Available: http://thethirdteacherplus.com/ (accessed January 5, 2016).

Capra, Fritjof. 1996. *The Web of Life*. New York, NY: Anchor Books.

Canadian Library Association (CLA). 2014a. *Leading Learning Bibliography*. Canadian Voices for School Libraries. Available: cvsl.ca (accessed June 21, 2016).

Canadian Library Association (CLA). 2014b. *Leading Learning: Standards of Practice for School Library Learning Commons in Canada*. Canadian Voices for School Libraries. Available: cvsl.ca (accessed June 21, 2016).

Canadian Voices for School Libraries. 2016. Home Page. Available: cvsl.ca (accessed June 21, 2016).

Central Okanagan School District. 2013. "GMS Human Library." Available: http:// www.gms.sd23.bc.ca/AnalyticsReports/Human%20Library%20GMS%2012.13.pdf (accessed January 1, 2016).

Central Okanagan School District. 2015. "École KLO Middle School—Human Library." Available: http://www.sd23.bc.ca/DistrictInfo/newsreleases/Documents/KLO%20 Human%20Library%20-%20April%2023,%202015.pdf (accessed January 1, 2016).

Cicchetti, Robin. 2010. "Concord-Carlisle Transitions to a Learning Commons." *Teacher Librarian: The Journal for School Library Professionals* 37 (3): 52–58. Available: https:// sites.google.com/a/teacherlibrarian.com/teacher-librarian-learning-commons-collection /home-rev (accessed January 1, 2016).

Council of State School Library Consultants. 2016. Standards. Available: https://cosslc .wikispaces.com/Standards (accessed January 1, 2016).

Derry, Bill, David V. Loertscher, and Leslie Preddy. 2013. uTEC Maker Model. Available: https://sites.google.com/site/yearofthelearningcommons/take-aways (accessed January 1, 2016).

Domeier de Suarez, Lisa. 2012, May 22. "Guiding Principles for the Learning Commons Grant Program" [Slideshare]. Available: http://www.slideshare.net/lmdsuarez /learning-commons-grant-application-2012 (accessed January 1, 2016).

DuFour, Richard, Rebecca DuFour, Robert Eaker, and Gayle Karhnek. 2004. *Whatever It Takes: How Professional Learning Communities Respond When Kids Don't Learn*. Bloomington, IN: National Educational Services.

Eaker, Robert, Richard DuFour, and Rebecca DuFour. 2002. *Getting Started: Reculturing Schools to Become Professional Learning Communities*. Bloomington, IN: National Educational Services.

Ekdahl, Moira, and Sylvia Zubke, eds. 2014. *From School Library to Library Learning Commons: A Pro-Active Model for Educational Change*. Vancouver, BC: British Columbia Teacher-Librarians Association (BCTLA). Available: http://bctf.ca/bctla/pub /documents/2014/SL2LLC.pdf (accessed January 1, 2016).

Fisch, Karl, Scott McLeod, and Jeff Brenman. 2014. "Did You Know? Shift Happens, 2014 Remix" [Video file]. Available: http://safeshare.tv/w/ntjwDrwEwh (accessed January 1, 2016).

Gladstone Library Learning Commons. 2012, November 26. "Human Library" [Web log post]. Available: https://gladstonelibrary.edublogs.org/2012/11/26/human-library/ (accessed January 1, 2016).

Greater Essex County District School Board. 2016. Collaborative Inquiry Reports. Available: https://publicboard.ca/Staff/Teachers/Pages/Action-Research-and-Collaborative-Inquiry.aspx (accessed April 30, 2016).

Grose, Derrick, ed. 2016. *School Libraries in Canada*. Canadian Voices for School Libraries. Available: cvsl.ca (accessed June 21, 2016).

Hamilton, Buffy. 2012, June 28. "Makerspaces, Participatory Learning, And Libraries" [Web log post]. Available: https://theunquietlibrarian.wordpress.com/2012/06/28/makerspaces-participatory-learning-and-libraries/ (accessed January 1, 2016).

Hamilton, Buffy, 2015. "The Unquiet Librarian—About" [Web log post]. Available: https://theunquietlibrarian.wordpress.com/about/ (accessed January 1, 2016).

Haycock, Ken. 2006. "Dual Use Libraries: Guidelines for Success." *Library Trends* 54 (4): 488–500.

Haycock, Ken. 2011. "Connecting British Columbia (Canada) School Libraries and Student Achievement: A Comparison of Higher and Lower Performing Schools with Similar Overall Funding." *School Libraries Worldwide* 17 (1): 37–50. Available: http://bctf.ca/bctla/pub/documents/2014/17-1haycock.pdf (accessed January 1, 2016).

Hellsten, Laurie-Ann M., Michelle Prytula, Althea Ebanks, and Hollis Lai. 2009. "Teacher Induction: Exploring Beginning Teacher Mentorship." *Canadian Journal of Education* 32 (4): 703–733. Available: http://www.csse-scee.ca/CJE/Articles/FullText/CJE32-4/CJE32-4-HellstenEtAl.pdf (accessed January 1, 2016).

Heltin, Llana. 2015, December 9. "How Literacy Programs and School Libraries Fare Under the New Federal Bill" [Web log post]. *Education Week*. Available: http://blogs.edweek.org/edweek/curriculum/2015/12/literacy_school_libraries_ESSA.html?cmp=eml-enl-eu-news3 (accessed January 1, 2016).

Henri, James, Lyn Hay, and Dianne Oberg. 2002. "An International Study on Principal Influence and Information Services in Schools: Synergy in Themes and Methods." *School Libraries Worldwide* 8 (1): 49–70.

Hyman, Shannon. 2014. "Planning and Creating a Library Learning Commons." *Teacher Librarian: The Journal for School Library Professionals* 41 (3): 16–21. Available: https://sites.google.com/a/teacherlibrarian.com/teacher-librarian-learning-commons-collection/home-rev (accessed January 1, 2016).

Indigo Love of Reading Foundation. 2016. Home Page. Available: http://www.loveofreading.org/en (accessed May 1, 2016).

International Association of School Librarianship (IASL). 2016. Home Page. Available: http://www.iasl-online.org/ (accessed January 1, 2016).

Kachel, Debra E., and Graduate Students of LSC 5530, Mansfield University. 2013. "School Library Research Summarized: A Graduate Class Project. Rev. Ed." Available: http://sl-it.mansfield.edu/current-students/school-library-impact-studies-project.cfm (accessed January 1, 2016).

Kamloops School District No. 73. 2013. "Beattie Library Upgrades 2013" [Video file]. Available: http://www3.sd73.bc.ca/general/content/school-libraries-are-transforming-21st-century-learning (accessed January 1, 2016).

Kennedy, Chris. 2015, February 12. "The Learning Commons Mindset" [Blog post]. The Culture of Yes. Available: http://cultureofyes.ca/2015/02/12/the-learning-commons-mindset/ (accessed January 1, 2016).

Knittel, S. 2012, September 8. "Acadia Junior High Donates a Drip Irrigation System to Tigithi Secondary School" [Video file]. Available: http://www.youtube.com/watch?v=qBb69wX9Q_s (accessed January 1, 2016).

Koechlin, Carol, Esther Rosenfeld, and David V. Loertscher. 2010. *Building a Learning Commons: A Guide for School Administrators and Learning Leadership Teams.* Salt Lake City, UT: Hi Willow Research and Publishing.

Koechlin, Carol, and Judith Sykes. 2014. "Canadian Libraries Leading Learning." Synergy, School Library Association of Victoria, Australia. Available: http://www.slav.vic.edu.au/synergy/volume-12-number-2-2014/perspectives-global/426-canadian-school-libraries-leading-learning.html (accessed January 1, 2016).

Koechlin, Carol, and Sandi Zwaan. 2014. *Q Tasks*, 2nd ed. Markham, ON: Pembroke Publishers.

Kompar, Fran. 2015. "Re-Imagining the School Library: The Learning Commons and Systemic Reform." *Teacher Librarian: The Journal for School Library Professionals* 42 (4): 20–24.

LaGarde, Jennifer. 2013, October 1. "Keeping Your Library Collection Smelling F.R.E.S.H!" [Web log post]. Available: http://www.librarygirl.net/2013/10/keeping-your-library-collection.html (accessed January 1, 2016).

Lance, Keith Curry. 2015. "4th Colorado School Library Study Cited in Education Week." Available: http://keithcurrylance.com/ (accessed January 1, 2016).

Levitov, Deborah D., and Christie Kaaland, eds. 2016. *Teacher Librarian: The Journal for School Library Professionals.* Bowie, MD: E L Kurdyla Publishing LLC. http://www.teacherlibrarian.com/ (accessed January 1, 2016).

Lexington School District One. 2015. "Learning Commons." Available: http://www.lexington1.net/academics/learning-commons (accessed January 1, 2016).

Library Research Service. 2013. "School Libraries Impact Studies." Retrieved from http://www.lrs.org/data-tools/school-libraries/impact-studies/ (accessed January 1, 2016).

Lippincott, Joan K., and Stacey Greenwell. 2011. "7 Things You Should Know about the Modern Learning Commons." Educause. Available: http://www.educause.edu/library/resources/7-things-you-should-know-about-modern-learning-commons (accessed January 1, 2016).

Loertscher, David V. 2008. "Flip This Library: School Libraries Need a Revolution." *School Library Journal* 54 (11): 46–48. Available: http://www.slj.com/2008/11/sljarchives/flip-this-library-school-libraries-need-a-revolution/#_ (accessed January 1, 2016).

Loertscher, David V. 2014. "Collaboration and Co-teaching—A New Measure of Impact." *Teacher Librarian: The Journal for School Library Professionals* 42 (2): 8–19.

Loertscher, David V., ed. 2015a. *The Library Learning Commons—Start a Revolution: Papers of the Treasure Mountain Research Retreat #22.* Salt Lake City, UT: Learning Commons Press.

Loertscher, David V. 2015b. "The Virtual Makerspace: A New Possibility." *Teacher Librarian: The Journal for School Library Professionals* 43(1): 50–51.

Loertscher, David V. 2015c. Treasure Mountain Research Retreat. Available: https://sites.google.com/site/treasuremtresearchretreat/home (accessed January 1, 2016).

Loertscher, David V., and Carol Koechlin. 2011. "Dear Teachers: The Learning Commons and the Future of Learning." *Teacher Librarian: The Journal for School Library Professionals* 39 (4): 51–54.

Loertscher, David V., and Carol Koechlin. 2012. "The Virtual Learning Commons and School Improvement." *Teacher Librarian: The Journal for School Library Professionals* 39 (6): 20–24.

Loertscher, David V., and Carol Koechlin. 2014. "Climbing to Excellence: Defining Characteristics of Successful Learning Commons." *Knowledge Quest* 42 (4): 14–15. Chicago, IL: American Library Association (ALA). Available: http://www.ala.org /aasl/sites/ala.org.aasl/files/content/aaslpubsandjournals/knowledgequest/docs/KQ _MarApr14_ClimbingtoExcellence.pdf (accessed January 1, 2016).

Loertscher, David V., and Carol Koechlin, eds. 2015a. *Coteaching and Collaboration: How and Why Two Heads Are Better Than One.* Salt Lake City, UT: LMC Source.

Loertscher, David V., and Carol Koechlin. 2015b. *The Elementary School Learning Commons: A Manual.* Salt Lake City, UT: LMC Source.

Loertscher, David V., and Carol Koechlin. 2015c. *The Secondary School Learning Commons: A Manual.* Salt Lake City, UT: LMC Source.

Loertscher, David V., and Carol Koechlin. 2016a. learningcommons. Available: https:// sites.google.com/site/schoollearningcommons/ (accessed January 1, 2016).

Loertscher, David V., and Carol Koechlin. 2016b. "The Year of the Learning Commons." Available: https://sites.google.com/site/yearofthelearningcommons/ (accessed April 30, 2016).

Loertscher, David V., Carol Koechlin, and Esther Rosenfeld. 2012. *The Virtual Learning Commons.* Salt Lake City, UT: Learning Commons Press.

Loertscher, David, Carol Koechlin, and Sandi Zwaan. 2008. *The New Learning Commons: Where Learners Win! Reinventing School Libraries and Computer Labs.* Salt Lake City, UT: Hi Willow Research and Publishing.

Loertscher, David, Carol Koechlin, and Sandi Zwaan. 2011a. *Beyond Bird Units! Thinking and Understanding in Information-Rich and Technology-Rich Environments, Refresh Edition.* Salt Lake City, UT: Hi Willow Research and Publishing.

Loertscher, David, Carol Koechlin, and Sandi Zwaan. 2011b. *The New Learning Commons: Where Learners Win! Reinventing School Libraries and Computer Labs, 2nd Ed.* Salt Lake City, UT: Hi Willow Research and Publishing.

Loertscher, David. V., Leslie Preddy, and Bill Derry. 2013. "Makerspaces in the School Library Learning Commons and the uTEC Maker Model." *Teacher Librarian: The Journal for School Library Professionals* 41(2): 48–51.

Lunny, Jennifer, and Dominique Sullivan. 2014, July 28. "Imagine the Possibilities" [Video File]. Available: https://www.youtube.com/watch?v=A_QnbQxnNCI&feature=youtu .be (accessed January 1, 2016).

Lynch, Matthew. 2015, September 15. "8 Ways to Rescue Public School Libraries from Becoming Obsolete" [Web log post]. Available: http://blogs.edweek.org /edweek/education_futures/2015/09/8_ways_to_rescue_public_school_libraries _from_becoming_obsolete.html?cmp=eml-enl-eu-news3 (accessed January 1, 2016).

Maliszewski, Diana. 2016. "Climbing Mountains: Methods for Mentoring Teacher-Librarians." Available: https://sites.google.com/site/treasuremountaincanada4/-building -a-learning-community/maliszewski (accessed April 27, 2016).

Marcoux, Elizabeth. 2015. "Technology and the Learning Commons." *Teacher Librarian: The Journal for School Library Professionals* 42 (5): pp. 65–66.

Marston, Natalie. 2002. "6 Steps to Successful Co-teaching: Helping Special and Regular Education Teachers Work Together." National Education Association. Available: http:// www.nea.org/tools/6-steps-to-successful-co-teaching.html (accessed January 1, 2016).

Maine State Library. 2015. Mentors for School Areas of Interest. Available: http://www.maine.gov/msl/libs/ce/mentor/mentors-schools.shtml (accessed January 1, 2016).

Massachusetts School Library Association (MSLA). 2015. Standards and Rubrics for School Libraries. Available: http://www.maschoolibraries.org/standards-and-rubrics-for-school-libraries.html (accessed January 1, 2016).

McVittie, Cecile, and Randy Duggan. 2014. "K-12 Learning Commons." *ETEC 510*. Available: http://etec.ctlt.ubc.ca/510wiki/K-12_Learning_Commons (accessed January 1, 2016).

Miller, Greg. 2013, October 27. "At Heart, I'm Still a Teacher" [Web log post]. Available: http://gregmillerprincipal.com/tag/learning-commons/ (accessed January 1, 2016).

Murvosh, Marta. 2013. "Follow the Leaders: Washington State's Stellar Advocacy Model." *School Library Journal*. Available: http://www.slj.com/2013/10/feature-articles/follow-the-leaders-washington-states-stellar-advocacy-model/#_ (accessed May 1, 2016).

National Education Association (NEA). 2015a. "New Policy Statement on Teacher Evaluation and Accountability—Adopted as Amended." Available: http://www.nea.org/grants/46326.htm (accessed April 30, 2016).

National Education Association (NEA). 2015b. "Tools and Ideas for Classroom Teachers." Available: http://www.nea.org/home/ToolsAndIdeas.html (accessed April 30, 2016).

National Governors Association Center for Best Practices and Council of Chief State School Officers (CCSSO). 2016. Common Core State Standards Initiative. Washington, D.C.: National Governors Association Center for Best Practices, Council of Chief State School Officers. Available: http://www.corestandards.org/ (accessed January 1, 2016).

New Jersey Association of School Librarians (NJASL). 2013. Mentoring. Available: http://www.njasl.org/Mentoring (accessed January 1, 2016).

NGSS Lead States. 2015. Next Generation Science Standards: For States, By States. Available: http://www.nextgenscience.org/ (accessed January 1, 2016).

Oberg, Dianne. 2014a. "Ignoring the Evidence: Another Decade of Decline for School Libraries." *Education Canada*, 54 (1). Available: http://www.cea-ace.ca/education-canada/article/ignoring-evidence-another-decade-decline-school-libraries (accessed January 1, 2016).

Oberg, Dianne. 2014b. "Relentlessly Focused on Learning: The Role of Evaluation." Available: https://sites.google.com/site/treasuremountaincanada3/advancing-the-learning-community/oberg (accessed January 1, 2016).

Ontario Leadership Strategy. 2011. Leadership Development: Mentoring. Available: http://www.edu.gov.on.ca/eng/policyfunding/leadership/mentoring.html (accessed January 1, 2016).

Ontario School Library Association. 2003. *The Teacher Librarian's Toolkit for Evidence-Based Practice*. Available: http://www.accessola.com/osla/toolkit/intro.html (accessed January 1, 2016).

Ontario School Library Association. 2010. *Together for Learning: School Libraries and the Emergence of the Learning Commons*. Toronto, ON: Ontario School Library Association. Available: http://www.accessola.org/web/OLA/Together_for_Learning/T4L_Vision_Document/OLA/OSLA/Together_for_Learning/T4L_Vision_Document.aspx?hkey=16f7cbb7-3556-4e39-a282-03fb29d202ad (accessed May 1, 2016).

Ontario Library Association. 2016. "Together for Learning." Available: http://www.accessola.org/web/OLA/Together_for_Learning/Welcome/OLA/OSLA/Together_for_Learning/Together_for_Learning.aspx?hkey=bd731cc1-48ef-4180-b80b-ddf3c39646d9 (accessed January 1, 2016).

OWP/P Architects, VS Furniture, and Bruce Mau Design. 2010. *The Third Teacher*. New York: Harry N. Abrams.

Parrott, Deborah J., and Karin J. Keith. 2015. "Three Heads Are Better Than One." *Teacher Librarian: The Journal for School Library Professionals* 42 (5): 12–18.

Ramsey, Karen. 2010. "The School Tech Squad: A Learning Commons Technology Boost." *Teacher Librarian: The Journal for School Library Professionals* 38 (1): 28–31. Available: https://sites.google.com/a/teacherlibrarian.com/teacher-librarian-learning -commons-collection/home-rev (accessed January 1, 2016).

Rendina, Diana. 2015. "Renovated Learning: Grant Resources" [Web log post]. Available: http://renovatedlearning.com/grant-resources/ (accessed January 1, 2016).

Reeves, Douglas B. 2004. *Accountability for Learning: How Teachers and School Leaders Can Take Charge*. Alexandria, VA: Association for Supervision and Curriculum Development (ASCD). Available: http://www.ascd.org/publications/books/104004.aspx (accessed January 1, 2016).

Reeves, Douglas B. 2008. *Reframing Teacher Leadership to Improve Your School*. Alexandria, VA: Association for Supervision and Curriculum Development (ASCD). http://www.ascd.org/publications/books/108012.aspx (accessed January 1, 2016).

Rixon, Gregg. 2014, October 15. "Inspiring the School Library" [Web log post]. Available: http://designinglibraries.org.uk/index.asp?PageID=526 (accessed January 1, 2016).

San Jose State University. 2015. School of Information: Teacher Librarian Program. Available: http://ischool.sjsu.edu/programs/teacher-librarian-program (accessed January 1, 2016).

Schultz-Jones, Barbara, and Dianne Oberg. 2015a. *Global Action on School Library Guidelines*. The Hague, Netherlands: De Gruyter Saur.

Schultz-Jones, Barbara, and Dianne Oberg, eds. 2015b. *IFLA School Library Guidelines, 2nd revised ed.* Available: http://www.ifla.org/publications/node/9512 (accessed January 1, 2016).

Scholastic Library Publishing. 2008, 3rd Ed. "Research Foundation Paper: School Libraries Work!" Available: http://www.scholastic.com/content/collateral_resources/pdf/s/slw3 _2008.pdf (accessed January 1, 2016).

Sobolik, Joanne, Elizabeth Russell, Holli Klatt, Debbie Thompson, Kim Jones, and Stephanie Wieczorek. 2014. "Exciting Times—A Transformation of Media Centers, Media Specialists, and Learning: A District's Philosophy." *Teacher Librarian: The Journal for School Library Professionals* 41 (4): 21–25. Available: https://sites.google .com/a/teacherlibrarian.com/teacher-librarian-learning-commons-collection/home -rev (accessed January 1, 2016).

South Dakota State Library. 2010. School Library Content Standards. Available: http:// library.sd.gov/LIB/SLC/#.VocTgShy90c (accessed January 1, 2016).

Steele, Ryan. 2015. "The Journey from Library to Learning Commons." *Teacher Librarian: The Journal for School Library Professionals* 42 (3): 12–17.

Sullivan, Margaret. 2011a. "Divine Design: How to Create the 21st-Century School Library of Your Dreams." *School Library Journal* Available: http://www.slj.com/2011/04 /sljarchives/divine-design-how-to-create-the-21st-century-school-library-of-your -dreams/#_ (accessed January 1, 2016).

Sullivan, Margaret. 2011b. "Walls Can Talk...But Are They Speaking to Teens?" *Teacher Librarian: The Journal for School Library Professionals* 39 (2): 13–15.

Sykes, Judith. 2002. "Accountability and School Libraries: The Principal's Viewpoint." *School Libraries in Canada* 22 (2): 1–33.

Sykes, Judith. 2006. *Brain-Friendly School Libraries.* Westport, CT: Libraries Unlimited.

Sykes, Judith. 2013. *Conducting Action Research to Evaluate Your School Library.* Santa Barbara, CA: Libraries Unlimited.

Sykes, Judith. 2014. "Moving Forward: Implementing and Sustaining the School Library Learning Commons (SLLC) Through Mentoring, Accountability, Research, Community (MARC)." Available: https://sites.google.com/site/treasuremountaincanada3 /cultivating-effective-instructional-design/sykes (accessed January 1, 2016).

Teacher Librarian: The Journal of School Library Professionals. 2014. Teacher Librarian Learning Commons Collection. Available: https://sites.google.com/a/teacherlibrarian .com/teacher-librarian-learning-commons-collection/home-rev (accessed January 1, 2016).

Texas State Library and Archives Commission. 2005. School Library Programs: Standards and Guidelines for Texas. Available: https://www.tsl.texas.gov/ld/schoollibs /index.html (accessed January 1, 2016).

Texas State Library and Archives Commission. 2016a. Talking Book Program. Available: https://www.tsl.texas.gov/tbp/index.html (accessed May 1, 2016).

Texas State Library and Archives Commission. 2016b. TexQuest. Available: http:// texquest.net/content.php?pid=601786&sid=5342381 (accessed January 1, 2016).

The Alberta Library (TAL). 2016. Online Reference Centre. Available: http://www .thealbertalibrary.ab.ca/services/online-reference-centre (accessed January 1, 2016).

Todd, Jordan. 2015. "St. Joseph High School Hosts Human Library." Ottawa Catholic School Board. Available: http://ocsb.ca/news/st-joseph-high-school-hosts-human -library (accessed January 1, 2016).

Todd, Ross. 2008. "The Evidence-Based Manifesto for School Librarians." *School Library Journal.* Available: http://www.slj.com/2008/04/sljarchives/the-evidence-based-manifesto -for-school-librarians/ (accessed January 1, 2016).

Todd, Ross. 2009. "School Librarianship and Evidence-Based Practice: Perspectives, Progress and Problems." *Evidence-Based Library and Information Practice.* Available: http://ejournals.library.ualberta.ca/index.php/EBLIP/article/view/4637/5318 (accessed January 1, 2016).

Treasure Mountain Canada (TMC). 2016. TMCanada. Available: https://sites.google.com /site/tmcanada3/tmc4 (accessed January 1, 2016).

Universal Mind. 2012. iBrainstorm. Available: http://www.ibrainstormapp.com/ (accessed January 1, 2016).

University of Alberta. 2016. Teacher-Librarianship by Distance Learning. Available: https://sites.google.com/a/ualberta.ca/tl-dl/ (accessed January 1, 2016).

Voices for School Libraries Network. 2016. *National Project: National Standards for School Libraries in Canada Project.* Available: https://sites.google.com/site/nationalslproject/ (accessed January 1, 2016).

Webb, Steven T., and Mark C. Ray. 2015. "Teacher Librarians: Mavens in a Digital Age." *School Administrator.* Available: http://www.aasa.org/content.aspx?id=37170 (accessed January 1, 2016).

Whelan, Debra Lau. 2008. "Three Spokane Moms Save Their School Library." *School Library Journal.* Available: http://www.slj.com/2008/09/sljarchives/three-spokane-moms -save-their-school-libraries/#_ (accessed January 1, 2016).

INDEX

AASL. *See* American Association of School Librarians

Accountability, xix, 45–46, 51, 120; for co-designing WSLLC goals and actions, 55–57; in library development, 51–53. *See also* Accountability resources; Accountability strategies

Accountability resources: "Assessing Effective School Library Commons Indicators: What Do They Look Like? What Questions Can Help Us Assess Where We Are?" 70–71; A Guide to Support Implementation: Essential Conditions, 64; *Leading Learning: Standards of Practice for School Library Learning Commons in Canada*, 59–62, 69–72; "Learning Standards and Common Core State Standards Crosswalk," 63–64; Professional Growth Plans, 69–70; "School Librarianship and Evidence-Based Practice: Perspectives, Progress and Problems," 72; *The Teacher Librarian's Toolkit for Evidence-Based Practice*, 67–69

Accountability strategies: The Big Picture, 63–64; Design and Document Instructional Strategies, 67–69; Evidence Collectors, 72; Introducing Standards through Symbols, 59–60, 61, 62; "Look-Fors," Strategies, Assessment Questions, 70–71; Professional Learning Goals, 69–70; Reflection, Evidence, Planning, 64–67; Where are We on the Learning Commons Journey?, 60–63; Where Do We See Ourselves in Evidence-Based Practice?, 72–73

Achieving Information Literacy: Standards for School Library Programs in Canada, 51

Action research. *See* Site-based action research

Alberta Library Consortium, 117

Alberta School Learning Commons Council (ASLC), 54–55

American Association of School Librarians, 6, 30, 50, 60, 62, 64, 80, 82, 104, 116. See also *Standards for the 21st-Century Learner*

American Library Association, 51

Andrea, Kevin, 11

ASLC (Alberta School Learning Commons Council), 54–55

"Assessing Effective School Library Commons Indicators: What Do They

Look Like? What Questions Can Help Us Assess Where We Are?" 70–71
Assessment for Learning Accountability Planner, 68
Assistive technology, 35

Bentheim, Christina A., 16
Best practices, 50, 79
Beyond Bird Units! Thinking and Understanding in Information-Rich and Technology-Rich Environments, 18, 20
Blogs, 84, 93, 94–95
Book studies, 92
Books, in the learning commons, 79
Breakfast club, 24, 26
British Columbia Teacher-Librarians Association (BCTLA), 85
Brooks Kirkland, Anita, 84
"By the Brooks" (blog), 84, 93, 94–95
"By the Brooks"—Libraries and Learning: Leadership for the School Library Learning Commons, 93, 94–95

Canada, school library standards in, 51–55. *See also* Treasure Mountain Canada
Canadian Federation of Library Associations, 51. *See also* Canadian Library Association; Canadian Voices for School Libraries
Canadian Library Association (CLA), 32, 51, 52
Canadian Voices for School Libraries (CVSL), 21–22, 53
Classroom teachers. *See* Teachers
Coaching, 7, 12–13, 39. *See also* Mentoring
Collaboration, xxi, 3–4, 7–8, 12–13, 39, 110; in data analysis, 46; in instructional design, 5–6; in libraries, 117–118; in the library learning commons, 63; in library commons transformation, 118–119; in planning, 5–6, 32, 47, 50; in research, 86, 88; with teacher-librarians, 9–10; in teaching, 8, 50; technology and, 82; in writing, 52. *See also* Co-teaching; Mentoring
Collaborative Library Policy (Alberta), 80
"Collaborative Teaching Recording Template," 22, 24, 25

Common Core standards, 56, 64
Common Core State Standards Initiative, 49–50
Communication, cross-school, 24, 26, 27
Community/ies, xx; of practice, 39–40; professional learning, 45–46; teacher-librarian, 112. *See also* Community engagement; Community resources; Community strategies
Community engagement, 109–110, 112, 115–120
Community resources: "Beattie Library Upgrades 2013," 128–129; "Concord-Carlisle Transitions to a Learning Commons," 129–130; "Did You Know? Shift Happens, 2014 Remix," 121–122; Guiding Principles for the Learning Commons Grant Program, 133–134; *Leading Learning*, 124–125; "Learning Commons in BC," 130; "Makerspaces in the School Library Learning Commons and the uTEC Maker Model," 127–128; "Pedagogical Shifts Inherent in the Learning Commons," 130–131; "Planning and Creating a Library Learning Commons," 129–130; "The School Tech Squad: A Learning Commons Technology Boost," 122–123; St. Joseph High School Hosts Human Library, 132–133; "Technology and the Learning Commons," 126–127
Community strategies: Changing Roles Reflections, 124–125; Circle Brainstorm, 130; Defining Our WSLLC, 126–127; Engaging Student through Making, 127–128; Finding More time to Engage Community in WSLLC, 122–124; How Does the WSLLC Pedagogical Shift Look in My Practice?, 130–131; Human Libraries, 132–133; Infomercials, 128–129; Introducing Change, 121–122; Write a WSLLC Proposal, 133–134; WSLLC in Ten Steps, 129–130
"Concord-Carlisle Transitions to a Learning Commons," 129–130
Conferences, 11, 30, 36, 40, 83, 85. *See also* Treasure Mountain Canada;

Treasure Mountain Research Retreat; Treasure Mountain United States

Consulting, 7, 12–13, 39; *see also* Mentoring

Co-planning. *See* Collaboration, in planning; Co-teaching

Co-teaching and Collaboration: How and Why Two Heads Are Better Than One, 17–18

Co-teaching, xxi, 8–9, 33, 35–37, 50, 52–53, 82, 83. *See also* Collaboration

Council of State School Library Consultants, 54

Curriculum: and mentoring, 21–22; standards for, 49–50. *See also* Standards

Data analysis. *See* Student learning data

Department heads, role of, 56

Department of Defense Education Activity (DoDEA), 49

"Did You Know? Shift Happens, 2014 Remix," 121–122

Digital needs, mentoring strategies for, 28

Distance mentoring, 17

"Divine Design: How to Create the 21st-Century School Library of Your Dreams," 96–97

E-books, 35

Educational assistants, 114

Every Student Succeeds Act (US), 51

Evidence-based practice, 48–49, 56, 72

Evidence-based research, 66, 68. *See also* Research

Experimental Learning Centers, 83

Facilitation, 7, 12–13, 39; *see also* Mentoring

Faculty. *See* Teachers

Feeder schools, coordination with, 5, 24, 26, 36, 37

From School Library to Library Learning Commons: A Pro-Active Model for Educational Change, 85–86

Gavigan, Karen, 86

Goals: for school development, 64; "SMART," 69–70

Grant proposals, 24, 26, 133–134

Greater Essex County District (Ontario), 88

Guidance counselors, 8, 55

A Guide to Support Implementation: Essential Conditions, 64–67

Hamilton, Buffy, 84

Human libraries, 132–133

IASL (International Association of School Librarianship), 30, 80

IFLA (International Federation of Library Associations and Institutions), 49

"Imagine the Possibilities," 20, 33

Infomercials, 128–129

Information Power, 6

Integrated instruction, 82

International Association of School Librarianship (IASL), 30, 80

International Federation of Library Associations and Institutions (IFLA), 49

Kachel, Debra E., 81, 99

Kennedy, Chris, 84

Kettle Moraine School District (Wisconsin), 24

Kindred spirits, 17–18, 19

Koechlin, Carol, 82–83, 92, 113

Kohout, Jessica, 86

Lance, Keith Curry, 81

Leadership, 66

Leading Learning: Standards of Practice for School Library Learning Commons in Canada, ix, xi, 32–33, 39–40, 51–53, 55, 59–62, 69–72, 80, 82, 85, 90, 93, 96, 119, 124–126

Learning commons: assessment of, 70–71; defined, 52, 86, 126–127; design of, 79, 96–97, 126–127, 129–130; funding for, 87, 89–90, 116, 133–134; goals and actions, 55–57; participants in, 55–57; research on, 83–84; resources for, 79; shared ownership of, 121; virtual, 35, 57

Learning commons literature, 77, 80, 81–82, 89

Learning commons pedagogy, xvii, 4, 10, 32–33, 48, 82, 113

Learning Commons Policy (Alberta), 54–55

Learning commons teachers: lead teachers, 56, 90; role of, 111–112, 125

Learning commons transformation, 32; funding for, 87, 89–90, 133–134; where to start, 90–91

Learning Commons website (learningcommons), 83, 92–93

Learning Commons wiki, 84

"Learning Standards and Common Core State Standards Crosswalk," 63–64

Lexington School District One (South Carolina), 86

Library collections, weeding, 33, 35, 79

Library commons. *See* Learning commons

Library programs, metaphors for, 78

Library Research Service, 80, 81

Library resources, online, 117

Library support staff, 33, 38, 114

Library technicians, 35, 39, 114, 125

Literacy programs, 51

Loertscher, David, 82–83, 85, 86–87, 90–91, 92, 101–102, 113

Maine State Library, 7

Makerspaces, 127–128

"Makerspaces in the School Library Learning Commons and the uTEC Maker Model," 127–128

MARC (Mentoring, Accountability, Research and Community), xviii–xx

Media specialists, 24, 26

Meetings, 30; agendas for, 47; appetizer, 92; breakfast, 24, 26

Mentoring, xix, 3–4, 120, 123; approaches to, 7; curricular, 21–22, 23; for digital needs, 28; distance, 17; by district networks, 11–12; goals for, 33; of library staff, 33; of and by principals, 5–6, 8–9, 34–38; by teacher-librarians, 9, 20–21, 31–33, 38–42; of teacher-librarians, 6–8; techspert, 26, 28. *See also* Mentorship case studies; Mentorship resources; Mentorship strategies

Mentoring, Accountability, Research, and Community (MARC), xviii–xx

Mentorship case studies: district teacher-librarian mentoring district, 38–40; principal as mentor, 34–36; principal mentoring other principals, 36–38; teacher-librarian as mentor, 31–33, 40–42

Mentorship resources: *Beyond Bird Units! Thinking and Understanding in Information-Rich and Technology-Rich Environments*, 18, 20 ; "Collaborative Teaching Recording Template," 22, 24, 25; conferences and meetings, 30; *Co-teaching and Collaboration: How and Why Two Heads Are Better Than One*, 17–18; "Exciting Times—A Transformation of Media Centers, Media Specialists, and Learning: A District's Philosophy," 24, 26, 27; "Imagine the Possibilities," 20, 33; "Mentorship of New Teacher-Librarians," 29–30; *School Libraries in Canada*, 21–22; Teacher Librarian Learning Commons Collection, 15–17; "Teacher Librarians: Mavens in a Digital Age," 26, 28

Mentorship strategies: Animating WSLLC, 20–21; Attend a Conference, 30; Continuous Commons Breakfast Club, 24, 26; Curriculum Corners, 21–22, 23; Keeping Track, 22, 24, 25; Kindred Spirits, 17–18, 19; Mentors as Superheroes, 29–30; Techsperts, 26, 28; Theory to Practice, 15–17; A Think Model a Week, 18, 20

Miller, Greg, 10–11

National Education Association (NEA), 69

National Project: National Standards for School Libraries in Canada Project, 92–93

Network groups, 11–12, 17–18, 20–21, 29

Networks of practice, 11–12

New Jersey Association of School Librarians (NJASL), 6

The New Learning Commons: Where Learners Win! Reinventing School

Libraries and Computer Labs, 36, 81–82, 91–92

Next Generation Science Standards (NGSS), 49

Northern Gateway Public Schools (NGPS), 11

On-site action research, 103–105

Open Commons, 83

Parent involvement, 116

Parent-teacher associations (PTAs), 116, 122

Pedagogical shifts, 130–131. *See also* Learning commons pedagogy

"Pedagogical Shifts Inherent in the Learning Commons," 130–131

"Planning and Creating a Library Learning Commons," 129–130

Principals: mentoring of and by, 5–6, 8–9, 34–38; role of, xvii, xxi, 4–5, 10–11, 12, 48, 55, 64, 105, 119, 125; and the steering team, 110–111

Professional development, 4, 30, 41, 47, 61, 67, 69–70, 87

Professional learning community work, 45–46

Professional learning teams, 47

Public libraries, school-housed, 117–118

Reading and research resources: Book Study—Make It Appetizing!, 91–92; "By the Brooks"—Libraries and Learning: Leadership for the School Library Learning Commons, 93, 94–95; *Conducting Action Research to Evaluate Your School Library*, 103–104; "Divine Design: How to Create the 21st-Century School Library of Your Dreams," 96–97; "Flip This Library: School Libraries Need a Revolution," 90–91; *Leading Learning Bibliography*, 93, 96; *National Project: National Standards for School Libraries in Canada Project*, 92–93; *The New Learning Commons: Where Learners Win!* 91–92; "School Library Research Summarized: A Graduate Class Project," 99–100;

Together for Learning, 97–99; "Transforming Library Spaces," 96–97; Treasure Mountain Research Retreat and Treasure Mountain Canada, 101–102; "Year of the Learning Commons," 102–103

Reading and research strategies: Blog study, 93, 94, 95; Color-Coordinating Literature and Research, 93, 96; Conduct a Website Study with "Cookies," 92–93; Introducing the WSLLC—Gathering Thoughts, 90–91; Join In—Take Away!, 102–103; Mini Treasure Mountain, 101–102; Participatory Learning "Architects," 96–97; Research Poster Art, 99–100; Study Your Own School, 103–105; Virtual Scavenger Hunt, 97–99

Record keeping, 22, 24, 25

Reeves, Douglas, 103

Reference materials, 35

Research, xix–xx, 66; collaborative inquiry, 9, 88; evidence-based, 66, 68; learning commons, 83–84; site-based action, 87–88, 89. *See also* Reading and research resources; Reading and research strategies

"Research Foundation Paper: School Libraries Work!" 80

Resources, for students and staff, 66. *See also* Accountability resources; Community resources; Mentorship resources; Reading and research resources

School administrators, role of, 12, 55–56, 105; *see also* Principals

School Learning Commons International Registry, 102

"School Librarianship and Evidence-Based Practice: Perspectives, Progress and Problems," 72

School Libraries in Canada (website), 21–22, 51

School Library Advisory Committee, 52

School Library and Information Technologies Graduate Program (Mansfield University), 81, 99

School library associations, 80, 85
School library impact studies, 80
School library learning commons. *See*
    Learning commons
"School Library Research Summarized: A
    Graduate Class Project," 99–100
School library research, 77–78, 80–81
School Library Resource Center
    (SLRC), 86
Schools in case studies: district-wide
    system, 38–40; innovative grades
    8–12, 40–42; small elementary, 34–36;
    urban high school, 36–38; urban K–9,
    31–33
"The School Tech Squad: A Learning
    Commons Technology Boost,"
    122–123
Site-based action research, 87–88, 89. *See
    also* Research
"SMART" goals, 69–70
Specialist teachers, 56
Standardized test data, 47
Standards: AASL learner standards,
    50, 60, 62, 64, 80, 116; alignment
    with, 49–50, 65; Common Core, 56,
    64; curriculum, 49–50; for learning
    commons development, 52–53; for
    school libraries, 51; introducing
    through symbols, 59–60, 61, 62
Standards for the 21st-Century Learner, 50,
    60, 62, 64, 80, 116
Steering teams, xviii, 29, 33, 34, 36,
    37–39, 62, 66; community participation
    in, 110; constituency of, 110–111,
    113–116; duties and involvement of,
    116–117; resource for, 17; roles and
    reflections, 48, 124–125
Strategies. *See* Accountability strategies;
    Community strategies; Mentorship
    strategies; Reading and research
    strategies
Student learning data, xxi, 46, 55, 68, 78;
    analysis of, 64, 89; from standardized
    tests, 47
Students: and community engagement,
    115–116; engagement of, 32, 115–116,
    118; needs of, xxi; on the steering
    team, 115

Teacher-librarian communities, 112–113
Teacher Librarian Learning Commons
    Collection, 15–17
Teacher-librarians, xvii–xviii: action
    research by, 88; collaboration with,
    9–10; district, 38–40; elimination of,
    78; funding for, 90, 116; mentoring
    of, 6–8, 29–30; as mentors, 9, 20–21,
    31–33, 38–42; role of, 12, 48, 56,
    83–84, 105, 119, 125; shared, 90; and
    the steering team, 111–112; travelling
    or virtual, 90
*Teacher Librarian: The Journal of School
    Library Professionals*, 16, 36, 84
Teachers: common planning time for,
    9; engagement of, 91–93, 96, 97, 99,
    101–104; mentoring by, 21–22; role and
    expectations of, 12, 56, 104, 113, 125;
    specialist, 56; on the steering team, 113;
    surveying, 61–63. *See also* Learning
    commons teachers
Teacher-Technologists, 125
Teaching, collaborative. *See* Collaboration
Technologies: assistive, 35; collaborative,
    82
"Technology and the Learning
    Commons," 126–127
Technology support, 32
Texas State Library and Archives
    Commission, 117
TexQuest, 117
The Third Teacher, 96
Time management, 122–124
Timetables, flexible, 67
Todd, Ross, 48, 72
*Together for Learning: School Libraries and
    the Emergence of the Learning Commons*,
    85
Toronto (Ontario) District School Board
    (TDSB), 7
"Transforming Library Spaces," 96–97
Treasure Mountain Canada, 52, 70,
    84–85, 101–102
Treasure Mountain Research Retreat, 36,
    101–102
Treasure Mountain United States, 52,
    84–85
Triangulation of data, 46

United States: curriculum standards in, 49; school library standards in, 54. *See also* Treasure Mountain United States
University of British Columbia, 84
"The Unquiet Librarian" (blog), 36, 84
uTEC model, 127–128

Vice principals, role of, 55, 111
Virtual connections, 63
Virtual Learning Commons, 35, 57
Virtual scavenger hunt, 97–99
Vision, shared, 66

Voices for School Libraries Network, 52

Whole school library learning commons (WSLLC) pedagogy. *See* Learning commons pedagogy
Wikis, 84

"Year of the Learning Commons" (Loertscher and Koechlin), 83, 102–103
York University (Toronto), 7

Zwaan, Sandi, 82, 92

ABOUT THE AUTHOR

JUDITH ANNE SYKES, BEd, MDiploma, MEd, educational author and consultant, is a former teacher-librarian, district school library specialist, principal, and school library services manager for the Ministry of Education in Alberta, Canada. Sykes recently served as project coordinator/contributing writer of *Leading Learning: Standards of Practice for School Library Learning Commons in Canada 2014* for the Canadian Library Association, which received the Ontario Library Association President's Award for Exceptional Achievement. Her published works for Libraries Unlimited include *Library Centers: Teaching Information Literacy, Skills, and Processes K-6*; *Action Research: Practical Tips for Transforming Your School Library*; *Brain-Friendly School Libraries*; and *Conducting Action Research to Evaluate Your School Library*.